Always Stop at a Lemonade Stand

Empowering Student Independence

Copyright © by Dr. Matthew X. Joseph

First edition 2023

All rights reserved.

No part of this publication may be reproduced in any form, or by any means, electronic or mechanical, including photocopying, recording, or any information browsing, storage or retrieval system, without permission in writing from the publisher.

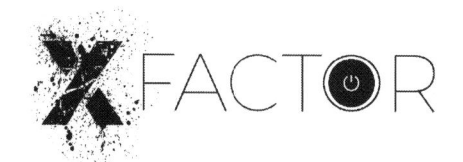

https://xfactoredu.org

X-Factor EDU

Our Mission Statement:

Be Unapologetically YOU

The journey to life-long independent learning begins in the classroom.

The Lightspeed Systems® suite of solutions for K-12 helps district administrators and educators support and empower students by providing a secure, safe and equitable learning ecosystem.

Lightspeed Filter™
Protect students from harmful online content wherever they are learning

Lightspeed Alert™
Identify students in crisis—before a critical event occurs

Lightspeed Digital Insight™
Gain full visibility and control of edtech use across your district

Lightspeed Classroom Management™
Keep students engaged and focused on digital learning

Lightspeed Mobile Device Management™
Ensure scalable and efficient learning device management

For more than twenty years, Lightspeed has been providing students the ability to explore with age appropriate guardrails.

Scan to learn more about Lightspeed Systems full-suite of edtech solutions.

Lightspeed Systems®
www.lightspeedsystems.com

©2023 Lightspeed Solutions, LLC. All rights reserved. Patents Approved. 2309

Table Of Contents

Foreword By Jennifer Womble 7

Life Lessons.. 14

Chapter 1: Always Stop at a Lemonade Stand 19

Chapter 2: Student Entrepreneurship 23

Chapter 3: Building a Diverse Classroom Community 33

Chapter 4: Cultivating Education for All Learners 39

Chapter 5: Curiosity Leads to Creativity 49

Chapter 6: Positive Learning Environment 55

Chapter 7: Student Participation vs. Engagement 63

Chapter 8: Building Self-Confidence................................ 73

Chapter 9: Nurturing Leadership Skills in Students 83

Chapter 10: Consumption to Student Creation 93

Chapter 11: Students as Creators of Content 111

Chapter 12: Lemonade Stand Moments for All 117

Chapter 13: The Paradigm Shift in Education 125

Chapter 14: Avenues for Student Independence 131

Chapter 15: Building a Student-Centered Classroom 179

Check out X-Factor Books 188

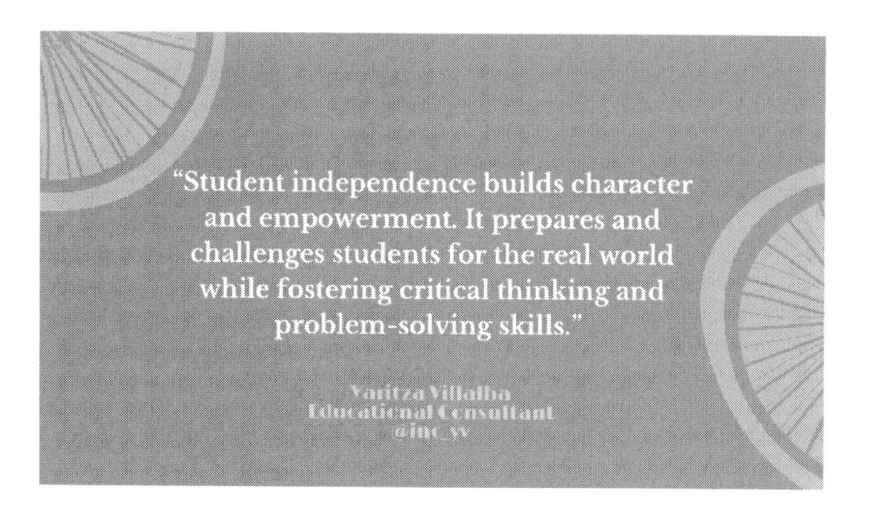

"Student independence builds character and empowerment. It prepares and challenges students for the real world while fostering critical thinking and problem-solving skills."

Yaritza Villalba
Educational Consultant
@mc_yv

Foreword

By Jennifer Womble

In the world of education, few individuals possess a remarkable blend of passion, expertise, and unwavering commitment to the cause of student empowerment quite like Dr. Matthew X. Joseph. An author, teacher, principal, and district leader, Dr. Joseph's journey through the realm of education has been nothing short of inspirational. It is an honor to introduce you to Dr. Joseph's transformative work *Always Stop at a Lemonade Stand: Empowering Student Independence*, a book encapsulating the essence of empowering student independence. This book is not just a testament to Dr. Joseph's illustrious career but also a guide to reimagining education for the future.

Understanding the rapidly evolving landscape of education is fascinating and imperative, where paradigms are shifting, and new horizons are constantly emerging. As someone deeply entrenched in education technology, I have always loved hearing presentations from passionate leaders who impact students and adults and aspire to share their energy with others. I have had the distinct pleasure of knowing Dr. Joseph as a fellow educator and guest on his podcast. In the realm of education, his name is synonymous with innovation, personalized learning, and a deep commitment to nurturing students' relationships and cognitive engagement. With great enthusiasm, I endorse this book and invite you to embark on a transformative expedition within its pages.

Dr. Joseph's career began in the classroom, where he understood that the most valuable asset in education is not the textbooks or technology but the students themselves. As a teacher, he recognized that every child has a unique curiosity waiting to be ignited. This innate desire to learn forms the cornerstone of his philosophy – that every student, given the right environment and guidance, can become an independent thinker.

From the classroom, Dr. Joseph took on the role of principal, where he renovated his school into a hub of innovation, and students were encouraged to question, explore, and experiment. This bold approach led to improved academic performance and instilled in students the confidence to take charge of their own learning.

What truly sets Dr. Joseph apart is his belief that empowerment is the cornerstone of education and that fostering meaningful relationships is key to unlocking the potential of every student. His work is driven by the profound understanding that when students are

Foreword

encouraged to experiment, discover creative outcomes, and take charge of their own learning, they become confident, autonomous individuals poised to shape a better future for all. He reminds us that education is not a one-size-fits-all endeavor; it is a dynamic, personalized journey that should be tailored to individual interests and strengths.

One of the most striking aspects of Dr. Joseph's work is his deep understanding of the symbiotic relationship between technology and education. In a world where digital tools abound, he firmly believes that technology should serve as a means to amplify the learning experience, not replace it. Through his efforts in integrating educational technology, Dr. Joseph has harnessed the power of digital tools to foster creativity, critical thinking, and collaboration among students.

Dr. Joseph's groundbreaking work challenges traditional notions of control in educational settings and offers a fresh perspective on cultivating innovation and independence in students.

Through the pages of this book, you will encounter a wealth of practical strategies and inspiring stories that showcase the transformative power of Dr. Joseph's approach. You will embark on a journey of discovery guided by an author whose passion for education is infectious. Dr. Joseph delves deep into the heart of what it means to nurture autonomous, inquisitive, and empowered students. He invites us to rethink the traditional paradigms of education, urging educators and learners alike to step outside their comfort zones, take risks, and embrace the endless possibilities for growth that surround us. You will gain a deeper understanding of how to encourage confident, independent, and creative students who are poised to shape a brighter future for all of us.

From classroom anecdotes to district-wide initiatives, his experiences will ignite your passion for fostering independent, confident, and creative students ready to embrace the challenges of the future. This book is not just a guide; it is a call to action for educators, parents, and anyone invested in the future of our society to rethink traditional notions of control and embrace the innate human desire for autonomy.

This book demonstrates that independence is not just a goal but a fundamental aspect of human nature. It promotes confidence, self-esteem, motivation, and resilience in our students, attributes that will serve them well as they navigate the world's complex challenges. It is a roadmap for educators and parents to empower the next generation of confident, self-reliant, and innovative individuals who will shape the future.

Dr. Joseph reminds us that education is not confined to the classroom walls. Learning happens everywhere, and it is a lifelong endeavor. He encourages us to embrace the idea that we are all learners, continually evolving and adapting. By modeling a love for learning ourselves, we inspire our students to do the same, not just during their formative years but throughout their lives.

Foreword

Educators and parents seeking to empower the next generation, I invite you to immerse yourself in the wisdom, insights, and inspiration that fill the pages of this book. Dr. Joseph's insight into the transformative power of education it is fueled by curiosity, guided by meaningful relationships, and focused on empowering students to become confident, autonomous, and creative thinkers. As you delve into the world of student independence and empowerment, you will find yourself inspired and equipped with the tools and knowledge to make a profound impact on the future of education.

Dr. Matthew Joseph, thank you for sharing your passion and your vision. Your dedication to empowering student independence is an inspiration to us all. May your words continue to ignite the flames of curiosity in the hearts of educators and students alike, lighting the path toward a brighter, more innovative, and inclusive world of learning.

Jennifer E. Womble

Chair, Future of Education Technology Conference

Always Stop at a Lemonade Stand
Empowering Student Independence

Nora from Millis, Massachusetts

Introduction
Life Lessons

Thank you for taking the time to pick up this book, however you got your hands on it.

Always Stop at a Lemonade Stand is my third solo book and sixth overall, and I am honored any time someone takes the time to learn from me and share my path. I've written many times about my childhood journey, growing up with my mom and sister since third grade. My mother, sister, aunts, and grandmother surrounded me, but that did not mean I didn't have a few male role models in my life. First and foremost, my uncle Tony Gibson was always there at my sporting events, listened to the "boyish" struggles, and was there when I needed him, when there were questions I didn't want to ask my mom or other women in my life.

He was the man in my life as a teenager when I needed it the most. He went out of his way to support and guide me and always reminded me to care for my mom.

Also my best friend Eddie Sherman's father, Eddie Senior (Big Ed), was a major influence in my life from sixth grade until high school graduation. Besides being a role model, he was my Uber before Uber. Because my mom was always working or caring for my sister, Mr. Sherman always drove me to practice. And yes, I called him Mr. Sherman even into my adult years. I spent many weekends and nights at the Sherman's pool goofing around and being teenagers with Eddie. Mr. Sherman treated me like his own, talked to me like a man, and showed me what it meant to be both funny and a family man. He also showed me how to treat women (he adored his wife Silvia) and that it is ok to be stern if done with love. Every time he dropped me off after high school football practice, his line was, "Do you think your mom left a note on the door to say don't come home?" He was a detective in our town and knew my father's troubles (Big Ed was probably the one who arrested him a few times), but he never treated me or my mom any differently. He was among the first people to tell me to "knock it off" when I acted immature and always told me I had potential and not to waste it. That was his way of telling me he knew about my dad and didn't go down that road. He always said, "You have way more to offer, kid; go prove me right." Well, I never got a chance to share some of my successes as an adult with him, but I know I wouldn't be where I am without that kick in the ass (and many more along the way from others).

And then there was Neil.

Neil Harrigan was a family friend before my parents split. He stayed much closer to us (my mom, sister, and me). By my elementary years, when my parents split, his kids were grown, and he enjoyed goofing around and staying young for Jenna and me. Neil and I would always go out and do things, mainly things that my mother wouldn't know about and definitely would not have approved of. Most notably, Neil let me drive his car at age 14, take his gun to a shooting range to shoot cans, and do other things that he probably wouldn't be able to get away with today. But this was the '80s, and that's what we did. When I was a teenager, he always took me to the movies. He either tried to set me up with a cashier and embarrass me or tried to sneak his hand over the counter and steal some candy, never successful, but he was never that sneaky and actually wanted to be caught to make me laugh.

But one lesson he always taught me, and one I took through my years as an elementary school teacher, principal, and now as a district leader, is to always stop at a lemonade stand. We'd be driving around aimlessly doing who knows what, going to a shooting range, trying to buy me cigarettes, etc. But if we saw a lemonade stand, we would always stop.

Whatever the amount was for a lemonade, he would give a five-dollar bill, and each of us would take a cup; he would make those kids smile for less than the cost of a cup of coffee. At first, I would say, "Neil, it was only a quarter; what are you doing?"

Neil was a small business owner who would look at me and say, "They didn't price it right. I paid what it was worth. Think about the effort it must've taken those kids to get there and set up. Then make some lemonade, then sit out, and sell it."

The bottom line for Neil, with random kids or with me, is that he wanted to help children experience the spark that comes with accomplishing a task that requires hard work. I've carried that message with me through all my experiences in education. I have not shared it often, but as my work continues to evolve and focus on student voice, independence, and empowering our learners, I knew it was time to share this story and other strategies to create student entrepreneurs and support building genuine confidence in young learners. You'll see that I also enlisted the help of fellow authors Laurie Guyon and Dr. Marialice B.F.X. Curran to give their own takes on how to create lemonade stand moments later in this book.

Confidence is the beginning to creating successful students.

When students are confident, they're willing to take risks in school. They're eager to push themselves and they have an innate desire to do so.

In a somewhat misguided attempt to boost students' confidence, we often award participation trophies to everyone. In my years in education, I've seen this kind of pampering lead to too many students relying on parents or teachers. When that happens, and the stakes get high, the student will turn and look for help instead of having the skills to push forward under pressure. When students have genuine confidence that has been earned, they can overcome missteps on their own.

This book will guide educators to empower students and help them develop the confidence to believe in themselves and the resiliency to push on when things get hard. I know I wouldn't be where I am today without some key people giving me a chance when I was a kid. Sometimes that was out of pity and sometimes I think they really saw something in me. In my senior year, my guidance counselor wrote in my college recommendation that I was a "diamond in the rough."

Thank you, Nancy Woitkoski. It is our turn to empower all students to be diamonds and to allow them to shine brightly and have their voices heard.

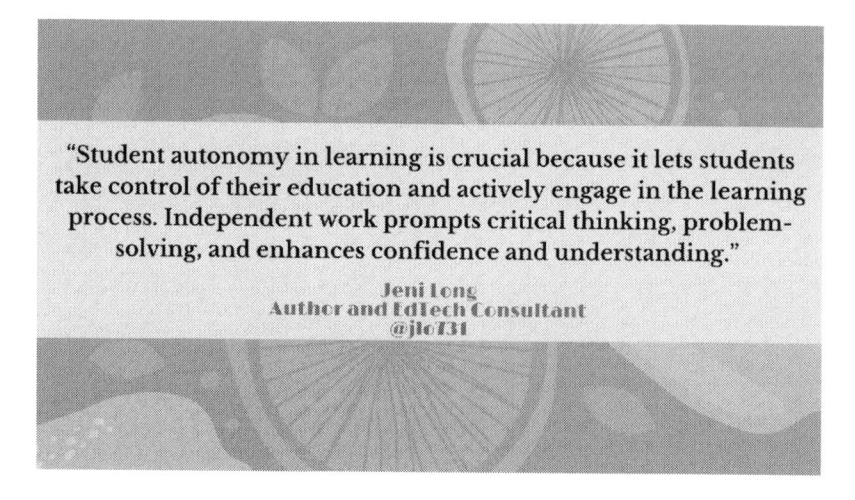

"Student autonomy in learning is crucial because it lets students take control of their education and actively engage in the learning process. Independent work prompts critical thinking, problem-solving, and enhances confidence and understanding."

Jeni Long
Author and EdTech Consultant
@jlo731

Chapter 1

Always Stop at A Lemonade Stand

Developing independent learning skills equips students with what they need to continue learning throughout their lives. In today's rapidly changing world, knowledge becomes outdated quickly and new information and technologies emerge constantly. Being independent learners allows individuals to adapt and stay relevant personally and professionally.

Students become more motivated and engaged when they take control of their learning. Rather than being passive recipients of information, independent learners actively seek out knowledge and are more likely to retain and apply what they have learned. This ability to take control and stay engaged with the world around them will help to develop a confidence that will serve your students well into adulthood.

Independence and confidence create student empowerment for several reasons. I want to stay true to the book title and start by sharing why creating a lemonade stand shows independence and essential skills that are helpful in the classroom. Neil never articulated these answers, but if someone asked me, *"Matt, why should we stop at a lemonade stand?"* I would answer with these points that tie in nicely with education.

Answer: *"It encourages entrepreneurship in kids."* Lemonade stands are often run by young children or teenagers learning about business and taking their first steps in entrepreneurship. By stopping at their stand, you can support their efforts, boosting their confidence and providing them with a positive experience.

Answer: *"It teaches kids life skills."* Running a lemonade stand involves various skills, such as budgeting, pricing, marketing, customer service, and communication. Stopping at a lemonade stand allows young entrepreneurs to practice and develop these essential life skills.

Answer: *"It will help kids build community connections."* Lemonade stands are often set up in residential neighborhoods, in parks, or at local events. By stopping and engaging with young entrepreneurs, you contribute to building a sense of community. You might meet your neighbors, strike up conversations, and develop connections with people in your local area.

Answer: *"We have to start instilling work ethic and responsibility into students."* By supporting young entrepreneurs, you help reinforce the values of hard work, responsibility, and dedication. The experience of running a lemonade stand can teach children the importance of commitment, perseverance, and taking pride in their work.

Answer: *"It definitely creates lasting memories for those kids."* Stopping at a lemonade stand can be a simple yet memorable experience for you and the young entrepreneurs. It offers an opportunity to interact with enthusiastic children, share stories, and enjoy a refreshing beverage.

These small interactions can positively impact both sides and create lasting memories. While it may not always be possible to stop at every lemonade stand you encounter, taking the time to acknowledge and appreciate the efforts of young entrepreneurs can make a significant difference in their lives.

So next time you see one, stop and watch those smiles. You never know what their potential could be; support it.

"As an educator my goal is to empower students to become life long learners. Regardless of what career they may go into, students really need to be confident in creative problem solving to be successful. The real world is filled with difficult problems that lack obvious solutions so it's essential that students have a methodology to take that on."

Tim Needles
Educator & Author of STEAM Power
@timneedles

Chapter 2

Student Entrepreneurship

Empowering students to be entrepreneurs involves providing them with the necessary knowledge, skills, resources, and support to develop an entrepreneurial mindset and pursue their own ideas and passions.

Encouraging creativity and problem-solving will foster a culture of ideas and innovation among students. Start by enabling students to think critically, identify problems or needs in their community, and develop creative solutions. Provide opportunities for brainstorming, idea generation, and collaborative projects.

Let's be clear: this book will not be about how to have young kids or students of any age start a business; it is to provide strategies for schools and teachers to create that level of independence and risk-taking in a classroom. The skills to be an entrepreneur are the same skills students need to be critical, independent thinkers and build confidence in learning.

As educators, we must focus on students' growth mindset and encourage them to embrace challenges. Enabling students to step out of their comfort zones and highlighting the importance of effort and perseverance in overcoming obstacles is one of the roles of a teacher. Overcoming difficulties will help change the perception of failure. One key to reframing challenges as opportunities is a school culture that values failure as a natural part of the learning process. This environment allows students to set achievable and measurable goals, breaking them down into smaller tasks to celebrate progress and maintain motivation.

In this shift to student risk-taking and empowerment, it is essential to recognize and leverage students' unique strengths and interests, providing opportunities for self-directed learning and tailoring teaching methods to accommodate diverse learning styles. Moving away from "sit and get" and moving toward fostering active participation in class discussions and activities by assigning group projects to promote collaboration and teamwork is the first of MANY steps in the instructional shift.

Building confidence and independence in students is a multifaceted process involving a combination of supportive environments, promoting a growth mindset, nurturing strengths, and developing self-reflection and self-efficacy. In my years as a principal and district leader, these strategies have been utilized by educators, parents, and communities to foster and enhance confidence in students:

Educate Students about Growth Mindset:

- Begin by introducing the concept of growth mindset to students.

- Explain that their abilities and intelligence are not fixed but can be developed through effort and effective strategies.
- Share inspiring examples of famous individuals who have succeeded through hard work and perseverance.

Normalize Mistakes and Failure:

- Help students understand that making mistakes and experiencing failure are natural parts of the learning process.
- Encourage them to see setbacks as opportunities for growth and learning rather than sources of discouragement.
- Share stories of resilience and perseverance to inspire them.

Encourage Effort and Persistence:

- Emphasize the importance of effort and persistence in achieving goals. Teach students that true mastery comes from consistent practice and dedication.
- Encourage them to set realistic goals, break them down into manageable steps, and celebrate small victories along the way.

Provide Constructive Feedback:

- Offer specific and constructive feedback to help students understand their strengths and areas for improvement.

- Focus on effort, strategies used, and progress made rather than solely on the end result.
- Encourage self-reflection and help students identify strategies to overcome challenges.

Foster a Supportive Environment:

- Create a safe and inclusive classroom or home environment where students feel comfortable taking risks and asking questions.
- Encourage collaboration and peer support so that students can learn from each other's experiences and perspectives.
- Celebrate the achievements and growth of each student, reinforcing the idea that everyone can improve with effort.

Teach Effective Learning Strategies:

- Equip students with effective learning strategies, such as goal-setting, time management, organization, and problem-solving skills.
- Show them how to break down complex tasks into smaller, manageable steps.
- Teach them to seek resources and support when needed, fostering independence and self-directed learning.

Finally, foster a **love for learning**. A love for learning comes from cultivating an engaging, relevant, and enjoyable classroom community. Incorporate hands-on activities, real-world applications, and student choice in the learning process. At the heart of learning is encouraging curiosity, critical thinking, and exploring different perspectives.

By implementing these strategies consistently, educators, parents, and communities can help build confidence in students, empowering them to thrive academically, personally, and eventually professionally. Confidence and independence are a foundation for their overall well-being, resilience, and success in various aspects of life.

You may have noticed that the bedrock for all of these strategies is having a growth mindset. Think of growth mindset as the seed, and critical-thinking and problem-solving as the treasured skills that will grow from it. These are valuable skill sets that every educator should aim to develop when encouraging entrepreneurs or independent thinkers. Critical thinking and problem-solving are not just academic exercises; they are skills that go well beyond the classroom and play a crucial role in shaping successful careers and fulfilling lives.

Critical thinking and problem-solving are twin pillars that underpin a student's journey toward becoming a well-rounded, adaptable, and successful individual. These skills transcend the confines of classrooms, textbooks, and exams, extending their influence into every facet of life.

Critical thinking involves analyzing, evaluating, and synthesizing information to form well-reasoned conclusions. It's about going beyond surface-level understanding and delving into a given situation's underlying concepts, assumptions, and implications. The ability to think critically empowers students to assess information and navigate complexities with discernment. It equips them with the mental agility to sift through a barrage of information in the digital age, discerning fact from fiction and making informed decisions. Moreover, critical thinking fosters the development of analytical prowess, enabling students to unravel intricate problems and approach them systematically. Students become active contributors to discussions, innovation, and positive change as they learn to evaluate evidence, consider multiple perspectives, and construct sound arguments.

Why cultivating critical thinking is essential for students:

- **Enhanced Learning:** Critical thinking encourages active engagement with the material, fostering deeper comprehension and knowledge retention.
- **Informed Decision-Making:** Students who think critically are better equipped to make informed decisions, whether it's choosing a major, selecting a career path, or making personal choices.
- **Problem Anticipation:** Students can anticipate potential challenges and devise proactive solutions by analyzing situations from various angles.
- **Effective Communication:** Critical thinkers are adept at articulating their thoughts clearly, making conveying ideas and collaborating easier.

Strategies for developing critical thinking:

- **Question Everything:** Encourage students to question assumptions, sources of information, and their own biases. Teach them to ask "why" and "how" to gain a deeper understanding.
- **Diverse Perspectives:** Expose students to a variety of viewpoints and disciplines. This helps them develop a broader perspective and adapt different thinking approaches.
- **Socratic Dialogue:** Engage in discussions that stimulate critical thinking by asking open-ended questions that prompt reflection and analysis.
- **Analyze Media and Information:** Teach students to evaluate sources for credibility, bias, and accuracy. This skill is crucial in the age of information overload.

In parallel, problem-solving is a life skill that empowers students to confront challenges and obstacles with resourcefulness and resilience. It involves creativity, adaptability, and persistence. Developing strong problem-solving skills enables students to navigate academic and real-world problems effectively. It encourages them to embrace setbacks as opportunities for growth, instilling a willingness to experiment, learn from failures, and iterate until success is achieved. Proficient problem-solving transcends memorization of formulae or procedures; it's about honing a mindset that seeks to dismantle problems into manageable components, generate creative solutions, and apply critical thinking to validate their effectiveness. The importance of problem-solving lies in its academic application and its universal relevance. From addressing personal dilemmas to tackling global issues, students armed with solid problem-solving skills can catalyze progress and contribute positively to their communities and the world at large.

Some essential components of problem-solving:

- **Define the Problem:** Help students break down complex issues into manageable parts. Defining the problem clearly is the first step towards finding a solution.
- **Brainstorming:** Encourage students to generate a wide range of ideas, even if they seem unconventional. Creative thinking often leads to innovative solutions.
- **Trial and Error:** Embrace failure as a stepping stone to success. Encourage students to learn from their mistakes and refine their approaches.
- **Collaboration:** Problem-solving is often more effective in a team setting. Collaborative efforts bring diverse perspectives and skill sets to the table.

Strategies for enhancing problem-solving skills:

- **Case Studies**: Present real-life scenarios that require students to analyze and propose solutions. This bridges the gap between theory and practical application.

- **Role Play:** Engage students in role-playing exercises that simulate challenging situations, allowing them to practice problem-solving in a controlled environment.
- **Project-Based Learning:** Assign projects that require students to tackle complex issues, fostering independent research and problem-solving.
- **Feedback Loop:** Provide constructive feedback on students' problem-solving approaches. This helps them refine their skills and strategies over time.

Critical thinking and problem-solving are not innate talents but skills that can be developed and honed with practice and dedication. Students who master these skills are better prepared to excel academically, adapt to a rapidly changing world, and make meaningful societal contributions. By embracing diverse perspectives, asking probing questions, and approaching challenges creatively, students can equip themselves with tools that will serve them well throughout their lives. As educators, mentors, and learners, let's prioritize cultivating these essential skills and empower the next generation to thrive in a complex and interconnected world.

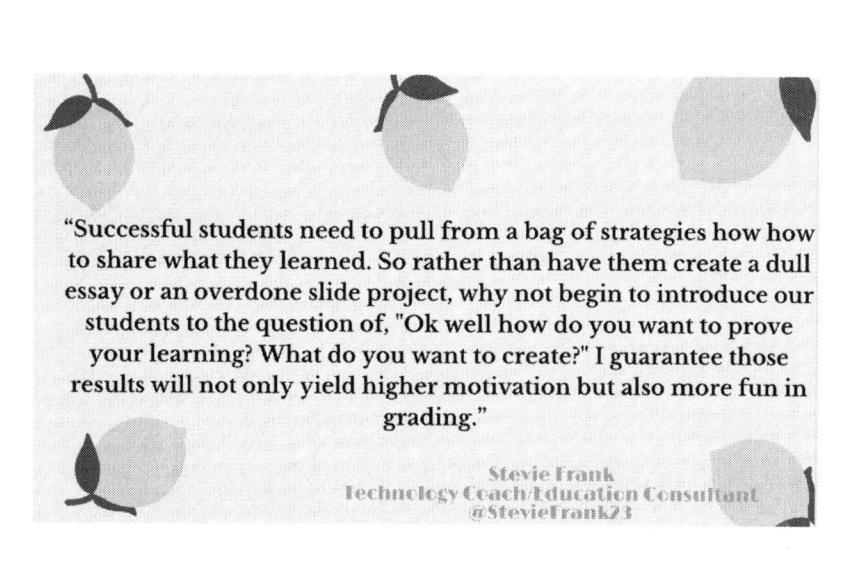

"Successful students need to pull from a bag of strategies how how to share what they learned. So rather than have them create a dull essay or an overdone slide project, why not begin to introduce our students to the question of, "Ok well how do you want to prove your learning? What do you want to create?" I guarantee those results will not only yield higher motivation but also more fun in grading."

Stevie Frank
Technology Coach/Education Consultant
@StevieFrank23

Chapter 3

Building a Diverse Classroom Community

Diversity and inclusion are essential components of a thriving educational environment. Keeping with the theme of the book, you ALWAYS stop. You don't drive by the kids at a stand because they use red instead of blue cups. Or they only have pink lemonade. Just like you wouldn't call on select kids, you call on ALL KIDS. A classroom that embraces diversity in all its forms and promotes inclusion reaps numerous benefits for students and society.

It is essential to build a classroom culture that reflects the real world. Society is inherently diverse, with individuals from various cultural, racial, ethnic, religious, socioeconomic, and ability backgrounds. A classroom that mirrors this diversity prepares students to navigate the complexities of the real world and interact effectively with people from different walks of life. Inclusive classrooms create opportunities for open dialogue about stereotypes, biases, and discrimination. Addressing these issues helps break down barriers and promotes a more equitable and just society.

A diverse classroom engages students with various perspectives, experiences, and ideas. Exposure to diverse viewpoints fosters critical thinking, stimulates discussion, and broadens students' horizons. Interacting with peers from different backgrounds helps students develop empathy and understanding. They learn to appreciate others' experiences, challenges, and perspectives, contributing to a more compassionate and inclusive society. Cultural competence is the ability to interact effectively with people from different cultures. A diverse classroom provides a space for students to develop this skill, which is increasingly valued in a globalized workforce.

Diverse classrooms encourage students to question assumptions, challenge stereotypes, and consider alternative viewpoints. This nurtures critical thinking skills that are essential for informed decision-making and problem-solving. In an interconnected world, collaborating and communicating across cultures is vital. Exposure to diversity in the classroom equips students with the skills and attitudes needed to become active and responsible global citizens.

Students from diverse backgrounds build relationships based on mutual respect and shared learning when interacting and collaborating. This contributes to stronger social cohesion and reduces feelings of isolation. Inclusive classrooms promote a sense of belonging among students, reducing bullying and exclusion. When students feel valued and accepted, they are more likely to contribute positively to the classroom community.

An inclusive classroom contributes to a positive school climate where students, teachers, and staff feel valued, respected, and supported.

Diversity and inclusion in classrooms are essential for nurturing well-rounded individuals prepared to thrive in a diverse and interconnected world. Beyond academic learning, the benefits of diversity and inclusion extend to fostering empathy, critical thinking, social cohesion, and the development of essential life skills. By cultivating an environment that celebrates differences, educators play a pivotal role in shaping future generations of compassionate, globally aware, and socially responsible citizens.

Creating a diverse classroom community is pivotal in promoting inclusive education and preparing students for the multicultural and interconnected world they will encounter. Here are some strategies to build and nurture a diverse classroom community:

- **Cultivate a Welcoming Environment:** Create a warm, inviting classroom atmosphere that celebrates diversity. Display posters, books, and artwork representing various cultures, languages, and backgrounds. This clearly conveys that diversity is valued and respected in the classroom.
- **Acknowledge and Respect Differences:** Initiate open discussions about cultural differences, race, ethnicity, religion, etc. Urge students to share their experiences, traditions,

and stories, fostering understanding and empathy among classmates.
- **Curriculum Inclusion:** Incorporate diverse perspectives and voices into the curriculum. Choose textbooks, reading materials, and teaching resources that reflect various cultures, identities, and historical events. This helps students see themselves and others in the content they study.
- **Collaborative Learning Activities:** Design group projects and activities encouraging students to work with peers from different backgrounds. Collaborative projects promote teamwork and allow students to learn from each other's strengths and perspectives.
- **Inclusive Language and Communication:** Use inclusive language that respects all students' identities. Avoid assumptions about names, genders, or backgrounds. Encourage students to learn and use one another's names correctly.
- **Celebrate Diversity:** Organize cultural festivals, heritage months, or events where students can share their cultural traditions, food, music, and art. These celebrations help students feel proud of their identities and provide opportunities for cross-cultural learning.
- **Mindful Seating Arrangements:** Consider seating arrangements that mix students from different backgrounds. This can help break cliques and encourage interactions among diverse peers.
- **Empower Student Leadership:** Create opportunities for student leadership roles that

promote diversity and inclusion. Student-led initiatives, clubs, or projects can help create a sense of ownership and commitment to fostering an inclusive community.
- **Family and Community Involvement:** Engage families and communities in building a diverse classroom. Invite parents and community members to share their expertise, cultural traditions, and stories with the students.

Regularly check in with students to gauge their feelings about the classroom environment. Encourage open dialogue about inclusion, diversity, and any challenges they face.

Building a diverse classroom community is an ongoing process that requires commitment, empathy, and a willingness to learn and adapt. By intentionally fostering an inclusive environment, educators empower students to become global citizens who value differences and collaborate effectively across diverse contexts.

"Student independence is crucial...
It equips learners with critical thinking
skills, the ability to self-direct their
learning, and confidence. This
independence fosters adaptability by
nurturing resilience, problem-solving
abilities, and effective communication,
making students better prepared to
navigate our ever-changing world."

Dr. Ariel Adrian
Reading Specialist, Long Island, NY
@drarieladrian

Chapter 4

Cultivating Education for All Learners

Like I said in the last chapter, you ALWAYS stop at the lemonade stand just like you ALWAYS focus on ALL students. In today's diverse and dynamic educational landscape, the Universal Design for Learning (UDL) concept has emerged as a robust framework to address all learners' unique needs and abilities. UDL is an educational approach that aims to create flexible, inclusive learning environments that accommodate students' diverse learning styles, strengths, and challenges. By acknowledging that learners vary in backgrounds, skills, interests, and learning preferences, UDL strives to provide equitable opportunities for all individuals to succeed academically and beyond. This chapter explores the principles, benefits, challenges, and implementation of UDL, highlighting its transformative potential in fostering inclusive education for all.

Using what I have learned as a teacher, principal, and district leader combined with deep diving into the UDL guidelines on the CAST website (https://udlguidelines.cast.org), I wanted to share that not only do we as educators need to design a diverse classroom, but we have to plan lessons for ALL students to allow them to reach their full potential.

Principles of Universal Design for Learning

UDL is rooted in three core principles: representation, engagement, and expression. These principles guide the design of instructional materials, activities, and assessments, making them accessible and effective for many learners.

- **Representation:** This principle provides multiple and varied ways of presenting information to students. It recognizes that learners have different preferences for perceiving and processing information. By offering content in various formats – such as text, visuals, audio, and multimedia – educators can ensure that students can access the material in ways that suit their learning styles and abilities.
- **Engagement:** Engagement is central to effective learning. UDL emphasizes the importance of offering diverse means of meeting that tap into students' interests and motivations. This could involve presenting content through real-world applications, incorporating interactive activities, and fostering collaboration among peers. Educators can keep learners motivated and invested in learning by providing multiple engagement options.
- **Expression:** The expression principle allows students to demonstrate their understanding and knowledge in ways that align with their strengths

and preferences. This may involve offering choices in how students can showcase their learning – through writing, speaking, creating, or using technology. By accommodating various modes of expression, UDL empowers students to showcase their learning in ways that best reflect their capabilities.

Benefits of Universal Design for Learning

The adoption of UDL offers many benefits to learners, educators, and the education system as a whole. UDL promotes an inclusive environment where every student, regardless of their background or abilities, can access and engage with the curriculum. It moves away from a one-size-fits-all approach, acknowledging that diversity is a strength to be embraced.

UDL aims to level the playing field by providing equal opportunities for success. It reduces barriers that might hinder certain students from fully participating in the learning process, thus promoting equitable outcomes.

By providing multiple pathways to learning, teachers can better address the diverse needs of their students. This not only supports struggling learners but also challenges those who excel. When learners are presented with content that aligns with their interests and preferences, their learning motivation increases. UDL's emphasis on engagement strategies keeps students more focused, curious, and excited about learning.

When we plan using a UDL lens, students can make choices that suit their learning styles, paces, and preferences, fostering a sense of ownership and autonomy over their education. Implementing UDL requires educators to explore new teaching methods and technologies. This can lead to professional growth, encouraging educators to improve their instructional practices continually.

Understanding and collaborating with individuals from diverse backgrounds is crucial in today's interconnected world. UDL prepares students to engage with a global society by fostering empathy, open-mindedness, and adaptability.

Challenges in Implementing Universal Design for Learning

While UDL holds immense promise, its implementation is not without challenges. Many educators need to become more familiar with UDL principles and how to apply them effectively. Comprehensive training and ongoing professional development are essential for successful implementation. Designing and delivering multiple formats of content, providing diverse engagement options, and accommodating various modes of expression can be resource-intensive. Schools and educators face time, technology, and funding limitations.

Traditional assessment methods might not align with UDL principles. Adapting assessment strategies to accommodate different ways of demonstrating understanding can be complex. Shifting from traditional teaching methods to a UDL approach requires a change in mindset and pedagogical practices. Some educators and institutions might be resistant to such a shift. In larger classrooms, fully customizing learning experiences for every student can be challenging. Striking a balance between individualization and practicality is important.

Implementation Strategies for UDL

Successful implementation of UDL involves careful planning and strategic execution. Educators should receive training on UDL principles and practical strategies. Workshops, webinars, and peer collaboration can aid in building a UDL-focused teaching community. Design curriculum with UDL principles in mind. Offer a variety of content formats, incorporate interactive elements, and provide choices for demonstrating learning.

Rethink assessment methods to allow for various modes of expression. Consider alternatives to traditional exams, such as project-based assessments or multimedia presentations. Leverage technology to enhance UDL implementation. Educational apps, online platforms, and assistive technologies can support diverse learning needs. Encourage educators to share their UDL experiences, strategies, and successes. Collaboration can inspire new approaches and refine existing ones.

Regularly assess the effectiveness of UDL strategies. Collect feedback from students and educators to make necessary adjustments. Universal Design for Learning is a transformative approach that celebrates diversity and fosters inclusive education. By focusing on representation, engagement, and expression, UDL empowers educators to create adaptable learning environments that cater to the needs of all learners. While challenges exist, the benefits of UDL far outweigh the difficulties. As educational institutions and educators embrace UDL principles and implement them effectively, they move closer to providing every student with an equitable and enriching learning experience. UDL is a beacon of educational progress in a world that thrives on diversity, ensuring no learner is left behind.

By embracing the principles of UDL, educators can create inclusive learning environments that accommodate various learning styles, abilities, and preferences.

Examples of How UDL Supports Learning

Addresses Diverse Learner Needs: Every student has unique strengths, challenges, and learning preferences. UDL acknowledges this diversity and aims to remove barriers that might hinder students from accessing and engaging with the curriculum. By offering various ways of representing content, multiple avenues for engagement, and diverse options for expression, UDL ensures that each learner can find a mode of learning that resonates with them.

Variety of Content Delivery: UDL encourages educators to present information in various formats – such as text, visuals, audio, and multimedia – to cater to different learning preferences. For example, providing a text-based explanation alongside visual diagrams and audio ensures that learners with various sensory preferences can grasp the content effectively.

Multiple Means of Engagement: Engagement is crucial for effective learning. UDL suggests incorporating diverse engagement strategies to tap into students' interests and motivations. This might involve using real-world examples, interactive simulations, collaborative activities, and incorporating students' passions into the curriculum. By allowing for choice and autonomy in how students engage with the material, UDL keeps learners more invested in their learning journey.

Variety in Transferring Learning: Students should be able to demonstrate their understanding in ways that align with their strengths and preferences. UDL provides students options for expressing themselves through writing, speaking, creating visual art, making videos, or using technology. This promotes a sense of ownership over their learning and allows them to showcase their knowledge and skills in ways that resonate with them.

Customized Learning Pathways: UDL encourages educators to offer flexible pathways to learning. This means students can progress through the material at their own pace and choose the best methods. For instance, some students prefer reading a text, while others benefit more from watching a video or engaging in a hands-on activity.

Reduces Barriers to Learning: Traditional educational approaches often inadvertently create barriers for certain groups of students, such as those with varied abilities or those from diverse cultural backgrounds. UDL aims to eliminate these barriers by making learning materials and activities accessible to everyone, regardless of their background or abilities.

Fosters Inclusivity: Inclusive education is at the heart of UDL. Educators create a more inclusive and welcoming classroom environment by designing learning experiences that cater to a wide range of learners. This not only benefits students with varied abilities but it also promotes a sense of belonging for all learners.

Increases Motivation and Engagement: Students' motivation to learn increases when presented with options that match their interests and preferences. UDL's emphasis on engagement strategies, active participation, and student choice keeps learners more engaged, curious, and enthusiastic.

Collaborating with individuals from diverse backgrounds is crucial in an interconnected global society. UDL prepares students for this reality by fostering empathy, open-mindedness, and adaptability through exposure to diverse learning experiences and perspectives.

UDL transforms education into a flexible and inclusive endeavor where every student can thrive, succeed, and contribute their unique talents to the world. UDL benefits students directly and enriches the teaching practice by encouraging educators to explore innovative methods and continuously improve their instructional strategies.

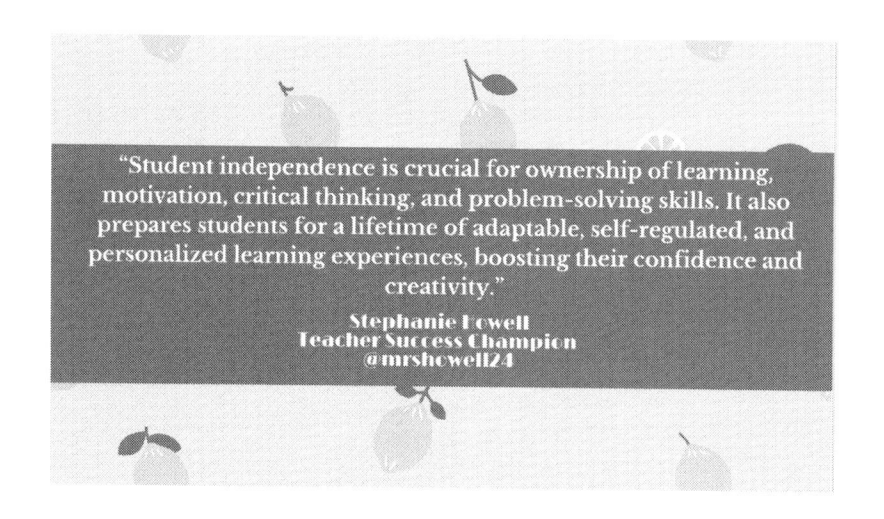

"Student independence is crucial for ownership of learning, motivation, critical thinking, and problem-solving skills. It also prepares students for a lifetime of adaptable, self-regulated, and personalized learning experiences, boosting their confidence and creativity."

Stephanie Howell
Teacher Success Champion
@mrshowell24

Chapter 5

Curiosity Leads to Creativity

Walt Disney said, "We keep moving forward, opening new doors, and doing new things, because we're curious, and curiosity keeps leading us down new paths." As someone who wrote many vision statements as a school leader, this quote sounds like one. However, student "curiosity" is one of those buzzwords we like to say in education but don't push for in schools. Why is that? We want students to be curious, but then we spoon-feed them what they should learn. We want "wonder," but all the agendas are posted and don't move off the lesson plan, "or else." Or else what? I always wondered that.

Building students' curiosity is a cornerstone of effective education. I describe curiosity as the engine of learning. By nurturing their innate desire to explore, question, and seek knowledge, we empower students to become lifelong learners, critical thinkers, and innovative problem solvers. Curiosity is the innate desire to understand the world and seek knowledge beyond what is presented. It is a catalyst that propels students beyond the confines of textbooks and conventional learning methods.

When naturally curious, students actively engage with their work, eagerly seeking answers and, in turn, delving deeper into topics. This proactive approach to learning not only aids in knowledge acquisition but also results in a deeper understanding of the subject matter. Curious students are more likely to ask questions, engage in discussions, and explore tangential topics, which broadens their intellectual horizons. When students are genuinely curious, their levels of concentration and attention increase. This heightened engagement leads to more meaningful interactions with the material, making the learning experience more enjoyable and memorable. Whether it's solving a complex math problem or delving into historical events, curiosity transforms passive learning into an active, immersive adventure.

Curious minds naturally question, analyze, and evaluate information and develop critical thinking and problem-solving skills. Building students' curiosity helps develop critical thinking skills as they actively seek to understand difficult concepts, weigh evidence, and make informed conclusions. Interest encourages students to explore multiple perspectives, consider alternative solutions, and develop creative problem-solving skills critical in real-world situations.

Encouraging self-directed learning empowers students to take charge of their learning journey. When students are curious, they become more self-directed and motivated to explore beyond the confines of the classroom. They seek out resources, ask thought-provoking questions, and pursue knowledge independently. This self-driven learning deepens their understanding and cultivates a sense of ownership and responsibility for their education. Curious students are willing to step out of their comfort zones, try new approaches, and learn from their mistakes. They understand that learning is a continuous process and are more resilient, adaptable, and open to personal and intellectual growth.

Curiosity and creativity are closely intertwined. When curious, students explore possibilities, connect seemingly unrelated ideas, and generate innovative solutions. By fostering curiosity, we provide fertile ground for students to unleash their imagination, think outside the box, and develop creative solutions to real-world problems. Curiosity fuels the drive to innovate and paves the way for future leaders and change-makers. Building students' curiosity is a cornerstone of effective education. By nurturing their innate desire to explore, question, and seek knowledge, we empower students to become lifelong learners, critical thinkers, and innovative problem solvers. Curiosity ignites the joy of learning, cultivates a growth mindset, encourages self-directed exploration, and stimulates creativity.

Creativity is not limited to just "specials" or "arts" in schools; it encompasses the ability to think critically, solve problems, and approach challenges from fresh perspectives. That includes ALL subjects. We empower students to become independent thinkers, lifelong learners, and future leaders by fostering creativity. Building a student's creativity is essential to keeping that "flame" alive. We often hear teachers say, "I saw IT in his eyes," or something similar, where the teacher knew the students were engaged and curious. That's where creativity starts.

Creativity encourages students to embrace their individuality and think differently. It inspires them to develop original ideas, question conventional wisdom, and challenge existing norms. By nurturing students' creativity, we create an environment that values diverse perspectives and encourages students to express themselves authentically. Creativity and critical thinking go hand in hand. When students engage in creative endeavors, they learn to analyze, evaluate, and synthesize information effectively. They develop the ability to connect seemingly unrelated concepts, identify patterns, and generate innovative solutions to complex problems. These critical thinking skills are indispensable in today's complex and interconnected world.

By cultivating creativity, we lay the foundation for future innovators. Creative students are more likely to envision untried solutions, invent groundbreaking technologies, and pioneer new approaches across various fields. Fostering innovation through creativity empowers students to shape the future and positively impact the world.

When students are encouraged to explore their creativity, they develop confidence in their abilities. Creative endeavors provide an outlet for self-expression, allowing students to communicate their thoughts, emotions, and experiences in unique and meaningful ways. This boosts their self-esteem, encourages risk-taking, and instills a sense of pride in their accomplishments.

Nurturing curiosity and creativity in students is a vital component of education in the 21st century. By evolving their creative potential, we equip students with the skills necessary for success in an ever-changing world. Through unique perspectives, critical thinking, innovation, boosted confidence, and adaptability, creative students become catalysts for positive change and shape the future with their ingenuity. Let us inspire and encourage curiosity and creativity in our students, for it is through interest that they will embark on a lifelong journey of discovery, growth, and intellectual fulfillment.

> Student independence is important because it fosters and supports students finding, refining, and fine tuning their likes and interests which in turn enables them to engage in society in ways that are productive, influential, and instrumental to the betterment of our world.
>
> Christine Delaney Bemis
> Educator
> @christinebemis2

Chapter 6

The Impact of a Positive Learning Environment

A positive learning environment is crucial in shaping students' educational journey. It encompasses a blend of physical, emotional, and social elements that contribute to a conducive atmosphere for learning and growth. This environment influences academic achievements and molds students' character, attitudes, and overall development.

Teachers play a pivotal role in shaping this environment. Their enthusiasm, empathy, and dedication are infectious, setting the tone for the classroom atmosphere. By fostering positive teacher-student relationships based on trust and mutual respect, educators become mentors who guide students academically, emotionally, and ethically.

When students feel valued, respected, and supported, they are more engaged in their learning. Teachers who exhibit patience, empathy, and a willingness to adapt their teaching methods to cater to different learning styles contribute to a positive educational experience.

A positive environment prioritizes students' social and emotional well-being. It helps create a safe space where students can express their feelings, share their thoughts, and build healthy relationships with peers and educators. When students feel safe, respected, and valued in their educational settings, they are more inclined to engage actively in their learning journey. A classroom where students are free from fear of judgment or ridicule becomes a space where they feel comfortable asking questions, expressing doubts, and sharing their viewpoints. This open discourse fosters deeper understanding and critical thinking, as students feel encouraged to challenge their assumptions and explore new perspectives.

At the heart of a positive learning environment lies psychological safety, and psychological safety is closely linked to motivation. When students feel comfortable, respected, and accepted, they are more likely to engage actively in their studies. Students who perceive their classroom environment as nonthreatening are more likely to be motivated to participate in class activities and take ownership of their learning. This intrinsic motivation is a powerful driving force that propels students to explore subjects beyond the curriculum, leading to broader intellectual development.

A positive learning environment profoundly impacts students' self-esteem and confidence. Educators providing positive reinforcement and acknowledging students' efforts bolsters their self-worth. Encouraging them to take risks and celebrating their achievements, no matter how small, instills a sense of accomplishment and pride. This sense of accomplishment isn't limited to academic success but also extends to personal growth.

Furthermore, a positive learning environment nurtures the habit of self-directed learning. As students become more self-assured, they become more willing to tackle challenges and overcome obstacles. Students become more adept at setting goals, seeking resources, and managing their time effectively. The fear of failure diminishes in a supportive environment, allowing students to embrace a growth mindset. They view setbacks as opportunities to learn and improve, enhancing their resilience and adaptability, indispensable qualities in an ever-changing world.

Education is not just about individual progress; it's about preparing students to thrive in a society that values collaboration and teamwork. A positive learning environment encourages social interaction and the development of essential interpersonal skills. Group activities, open dialogues, projects, and teamwork enable students to learn how to communicate, negotiate, and cooperate with their peers effectively. They learn to appreciate diverse perspectives, communicate effectively, and cooperate with peers. These skills extend beyond the classroom, preparing students for future professional endeavors and a globally interconnected world.

These collaborative experiences provide valuable life skills as students learn to work harmoniously with individuals from different backgrounds. These interactions lay the foundation for empathy and understanding, contributing to building a compassionate and interconnected society.

A positive learning environment is a breeding ground for critical thinking and creativity. When students can think critically, share unconventional ideas, and approach problems from multiple angles, they develop a deeper understanding of the subject matter. By questioning assumptions and analyzing information critically, they develop skills that transcend the classroom. Teachers who create this environment foster a generation of thinkers who are unafraid to challenge the status quo. This environment promotes innovation and equips students with the skills to adapt to an ever-evolving landscape.

Furthermore, creativity thrives in an atmosphere that encourages experimentation and risk-taking. When students are free to explore their unique problem-solving approaches, they develop a sense of agency and innovation. These skills equip students to tackle complex challenges in their academic pursuits and future careers.

Strategies for Cultivating a Positive Learning Environment

Creating a positive learning environment requires intentional efforts from educators, administrators, and other stakeholders. Here are effective strategies to foster a nurturing and uplifting educational setting:

Establish Clear Expectations: Set clear and consistent expectations for behavior, participation, and academic performance. Students who understand these expectations feel more confident and secure in their environment.

Build Positive Relationships: Cultivate positive relationships with students based on respect, empathy, and trust. Show genuine interest in their well-being and academic progress, and create opportunities for one-on-one interactions.

Promote Inclusivity: Celebrate diversity and create an inclusive environment where all students feel accepted and valued. Incorporate diverse perspectives, cultures, and experiences into the curriculum and classroom discussions.

Encourage Collaboration: Design activities and projects that encourage student collaboration and teamwork. Collaborative learning fosters a sense of belonging and allows students to learn from one another.

Offer Constructive Feedback: Provide timely and constructive feedback that focuses on students' strengths and areas for improvement. Constructive feedback helps students feel supported and motivated to continue learning.

Personalized Learning: Recognize that each student has unique learning styles and needs. Tailor your teaching methods to accommodate different learning preferences, ensuring every student can thrive.

Create a Safe Space: Establish a safe and non-judgmental environment where students feel comfortable expressing their opinions and asking questions. Encourage open dialogue and ensure that all voices are heard.

Use Positive Reinforcement: Acknowledge and celebrate students' big and small achievements. Positive reinforcement reinforces positive behavior and motivates students to continue striving for excellence.

Incorporate Hands-On Activities: Engage students with hands-on and interactive learning experiences. These activities make learning enjoyable and help students connect theoretical concepts to real-world applications.

Focus on Growth Mindset: Encourage a growth mindset where students believe their abilities can be developed through effort and learning. Teach them to embrace challenges as opportunities for growth rather than as obstacles.

Emphasize Self-Care: Educate students about the importance of self-care and well-being. Encourage them to manage their stress, take breaks, and engage in activities that promote relaxation.

A positive learning environment yields numerous benefits that extend to students' academic success and personal development such as:

Improved Academic Performance: Students in a positive learning environment are more motivated to learn, leading to better academic performance and achievement.

Enhanced Social Skills: Positive interactions and collaborative activities help students develop strong social skills, empathy, and the ability to work effectively in teams.

Increased Self-Esteem: A positive environment boosts students' self-esteem and self-confidence, encouraging them to take on challenges and pursue their goals.

Lifelong Love for Learning: Students who experience the joy of learning in a positive environment are more likely to develop a lifelong love for learning and curiosity about the world around them.

Emotional Resilience: A supportive environment equips students with emotional resilience and coping skills, enabling them to navigate challenges confidently.

Creating a positive learning environment is a collaborative effort that involves educators, administrators, parents, and students themselves. As educators and stakeholders invest in cultivating a positive learning environment, they contribute to the holistic development of students and lay the foundation for their future success in education, careers, and life as responsible and compassionate citizens.

A positive learning environment instills a love for learning that transcends formal education. When students are exposed to an environment that values curiosity, critical thinking, and exploration, they are more likely to seek knowledge long after leaving the classroom. It goes beyond academic success; it shapes character, fosters growth, and prepares students for a world that demands collaboration, critical thinking, and adaptability. A classroom prioritizing psychological safety, self-esteem, collaboration, critical thinking, and creativity lays the foundation for a lifetime of learning and personal development.

Chapter 7

Student Participation vs Engagement

In education, two essential concepts often discussed are student participation and engagement. Sometimes these terms are used interchangeably; however, they are very different. While both are crucial components of an effective learning environment, they possess distinct characteristics and implications. It is essential to grasp the nuances between these concepts to create a dynamic and enriching educational experience for students. This chapter will explore the differences between student participation and engagement, their impact on learning outcomes, and practical strategies to enhance both aspects in the classroom.

Student participation refers to students' involvement and contributions to various aspects of the educational process. It encompasses multiple activities, including class discussions, group work, sharing opinions, volunteering an answer, raising a hand, and completing in-class assignments.

Student participation is important for building an interactive learning experience in the classroom. Actively participating in class discussions allows students to express their ideas, share their perspectives, and engage in critical thinking. It fosters a collaborative learning environment where students can learn from each other and develop a deeper understanding of the subject matter. Teachers who encourage and value student participation create a safe space for students to voice their thoughts, which can boost their confidence and communication skills.

While classroom participation is a positive aspect of the learning process, it has limitations. Firstly, classroom participation may not accurately reflect a student's understanding of the subject matter. Some students may be more extroverted and confident in voicing their opinions, while others may be introverted or shy, leading to unequal participation. Quiet students who prefer to reflect and process information internally may have a deeper understanding of the material, but their lack of active participation may not showcase their knowledge adequately.

Secondly, the quality of participation matters more than the quantity. Merely speaking up in class does not guarantee a deep grasp of the concepts. Students may provide superficial answers or repeat information without truly comprehending it. In contrast, students who actively listen, take notes and reflect thoughtfully may demonstrate better learning outcomes, even if they don't participate as frequently. Moreover, some topics or learning styles may lend poorly to classroom discussions. Complex or abstract subjects require extended periods of individual study and research to internalize the material thoroughly. Additionally, some students may prefer alternative learning methods, such as hands-on activities, visual aids, or one-on-one discussions with teachers, which may not be fully reflected in classroom participation metrics.

Furthermore, classroom participation mainly focuses on verbal expression, which may only be the preferred or most effective mode of communication for some students. Some students prefer to process information internally, take notes, or engage in written reflections rather than actively participate in class discussions. Exclusively valuing verbal participation may overlook the valuable contributions of these students and fail to capture the full spectrum of their learning.

While participation is important, it only scratches the surface of deeper learning. Kids have learned how to "play school," give answers when needed, complete the worksheet, and then wait until the bell. Call and response questions are more for moving the lesson along than for developing deeper independent learning.

On the other hand, student engagement goes beyond mere participation and involves a deep emotional, behavioral, and cognitive connection to the learning process. It goes beyond mere compliance with academic requirements. Engaged students are intrinsically motivated, curious, and enthusiastic about their studies. They actively seek to understand the subject matter, apply knowledge to real-life situations, and exhibit higher-order thinking skills. It encompasses the level of interest, motivation, and dedication students display toward their studies and their involvement in various educational activities and interactions with peers, teachers, and the learning environment. Engaged students are more likely to be self-directed, motivated, and proactive in seeking knowledge and understanding.

Cognitive engagement involves students' mental investment in the learning process. It includes active listening, critical thinking, and connecting new information to existing knowledge. Engaged students are curious and ask questions to deepen their understanding rather than passively accepting information. They exhibit higher levels of concentration and retention of information due to their genuine interest in the subject matter. They are also more likely to persist in facing challenges and exhibit a growth mindset, viewing obstacles as opportunities to learn and grow.

Emotional engagement refers to the positive feelings and emotions associated with learning. When students feel a sense of belonging and emotional connection to the learning environment, they are more likely to be motivated to learn and achieve their academic goals. Positive emotions like joy, curiosity, and excitement significantly enhance motivation. They also create a supportive learning atmosphere and foster a love for learning.

Behavioral engagement relates to the active involvement of students in academic activities and their adherence to classroom rules and expectations. Engaged students participate in class discussions, collaborate with peers, and complete assignments on time. They are more likely to be present and attentive during lectures and participate in extracurricular activities that extend their learning beyond the traditional classroom setting.

Engaged students participate in class activities, complete assignments on time, and demonstrate a proactive study approach. Their actions demonstrate a commitment to learning and personal growth. Unlike classroom participation, which can be visible during specific moments in class, student engagement is a continuous and ongoing state. Engaged students are consistently motivated and invested in their learning inside and outside the classroom. Their engagement extends beyond formal class time and often includes independent study, seeking out additional resources, and pursuing learning opportunities beyond the curriculum.

Several factors influence student engagement. The teaching methods employed by educators play a crucial role in shaping the learning experience. Educators can implement various strategies to enhance student engagement, such as incorporating hands-on activities, providing opportunities for student choice and autonomy, offering real-world applications of the material, and incorporating technology to cater to different learning styles. Innovative and interactive teaching techniques like project-based learning and flipped classrooms also increase student engagement.

The relationship between teachers and students is also essential. Supportive and caring teachers interested in their student's well-being and academic progress can significantly impact student motivation and engagement.

Furthermore, the learning environment and school culture significantly influence student engagement. Schools that create a positive, inclusive, and stimulating atmosphere tend to foster higher levels of engagement among their students. Opportunities for student voice and agency, where students have a say in their learning experiences and can contribute to decision-making processes, also promote engagement.

Technology has played a crucial role in shaping student engagement in recent years. Digital tools and online platforms can offer personalized learning experiences catering to individual students' interests and needs, increasing their motivation and involvement in learning. However, digital worksheets fall into the "participation" lane because there is no active deep learning.

Educators should promote student engagement to foster meaningful learning experiences rather than relying solely on classroom participation. While encouraging participation is valuable, creating a learning environment that nurtures students' intrinsic motivation, curiosity, and emotional well-being is equally important.

Effective strategies that teachers can use to boost student engagement in the classroom:

Create a Positive Learning Environment: Establish a supportive and inclusive classroom culture where students feel safe to express their ideas and opinions without fear of judgment. Show genuine interest in their thoughts and experiences, and encourage mutual respect among students.

Use Active Learning Techniques: Incorporate active learning strategies that encourage students to participate actively in the learning process. These may include group discussions, debates, role-playing, hands-on activities, and problem-solving tasks.

Integrate Technology: Utilize educational technology tools to enhance learning experiences. Interactive presentations, educational apps, and multimedia resources can make lessons more engaging and cater to various learning styles.

Offer Student Choice: Provide opportunities for student choice and autonomy in their learning. Offer different project options, allow students to select topics of interest, and let them have a say in demonstrating their understanding of the material.

Connect Learning to Real-Life Contexts: Relate lessons to real-world scenarios to make the content more relevant and meaningful for students. Understanding the practical applications of their learning can increase their motivation and engagement.

Use Storytelling and Narratives: Incorporate storytelling techniques to present information compellingly and memorably. Narratives can captivate students' attention and make complex concepts more accessible.

Encourage Collaborative Learning: Promote group work and collaborative projects that require students to work together and learn from one another. Collaboration fosters teamwork, communication skills, and a sense of belonging within the classroom community.

Provide Timely Feedback: Offer prompt and constructive feedback to students on their work. Positive reinforcement and constructive criticism can motivate students to improve and actively participate in their learning progress.

Use Visual Resources: Utilize visual aids, such as charts, diagrams, and videos, to supplement verbal explanations. Visuals can reinforce understanding and help visual learners process information more effectively.

Incorporate Movement: Incorporate movement into the lessons, such as group activities that involve physical motion or opportunities for students to move around the classroom. Kinesthetic activities can help maintain students' focus and energy levels.

Set Clear Goals and Objectives: Communicate each lesson's learning objectives and expectations. When students understand what they are working towards, they are more likely to engage actively in the learning process.

Celebrate Achievements: Recognize and celebrate students' big and small accomplishments. Positive reinforcement and acknowledgment of their efforts can boost their confidence and motivation to continue learning.

Make Learning Fun: Infuse elements of fun and creativity into the classroom. Gamify lessons, use educational games and incorporate humor when appropriate to create an enjoyable learning atmosphere.

Student engagement is a fundamental aspect of effective education. Engaged students are more likely to succeed academically, develop critical thinking skills, and become lifelong learners. Educators, schools, and policymakers must work collaboratively to create an environment that fosters student engagement and cultivates a love for learning that extends far beyond the classroom walls. By nurturing engagement, we empower students to become active participants in their education and prepare them for a successful future in an ever-changing world.

> "Independence provides students with the freedom to explore the curiosity sparked by questions that emerge during the learning process. It fosters the development of critical thinking skills and allows for exploration. This allows students to better understand their own strengths and weaknesses, while also building confidence and taking ownership of their learning."
>
> Heather Brantley
> Educator - Lifetime Learner
> @heathertechedu

Chapter 8

Overcoming Challenges and Building Self Confidence

Education is a transformative journey through which individuals acquire knowledge, develop skills, and cultivate intellectual and personal growth. Yet, a student's educational journey is paved with challenges, ranging from grasping complex subjects to managing time efficiently and combating stress. These challenges, while daunting, hold immense value in the development of students. The ability to overcome challenges is an essential skill that not only propels academic success but also nurtures resilience, adaptability, and a lifelong passion for learning.

With the cultivation of resilience, students will find themselves with the ability to rebound from setbacks, adapt to new circumstances, and persist despite adversity. By navigating these challenges, students develop a resilient mindset that serves them well beyond academia, preparing them to tackle life's myriad of challenges.

The successful conquest of learning challenges also bolsters self-confidence. Each challenge surmounted becomes a testament to one's capabilities, fostering a sense of accomplishment and self-worth. This newfound confidence empowers students to confront even greater challenges with determination and poise.

Tackling academic challenges is an organic way to stimulate critical thinking and problem-solving abilities. Students learn to analyze situations, identify potential solutions, and make informed decisions. These skills transcend the classroom, equipping students to address real-world problems effectively.

Overcoming learning challenges also fosters a growth mindset, where students recognize their abilities can be honed through effort and dedication. This mindset shifts the focus from innate talent to the power of hard work, encouraging students to embrace challenges as opportunities for growth and learning.

The virtue of perseverance is honed through surmounting learning obstacles. Students who persevere in the face of difficulties exhibit strong work ethics and an unwavering commitment to their goals. This attribute is pivotal in achieving sustained success.

Strategies for Overcoming Learning Challenges

Effectively navigating learning challenges entails a combination of self-awareness, efficient study techniques, and proactive problem-solving.

The following strategies can guide students to surmount obstacles and thrive in their educational journey:

Self-Awareness and Reflection:

- Identify Specific Challenges: Acknowledge and articulate the precise areas or subjects posing challenges. Understanding the nature of obstacles is a crucial first step toward devising effective solutions.
- Assess Learning Styles: Reflect on your preferred learning style – whether visual, auditory, or kinesthetic. Tailor your study methods to align with your learning style for more efficient understanding and retention.
- Set Realistic Goals: Define attainable short-term and long-term goals. Breaking down intricate tasks into manageable steps enables you to monitor progress and sustain motivation.

Effective Study Techniques:

- Active Learning: Engage proactively with the material by summarizing, paraphrasing, and posing questions. This deepens understanding and enhances the retention of information.
- Time Management: Craft a study schedule that allocates time for each subject and task. Prioritize assignments based on importance and deadline, ensuring a balanced approach to learning.
- Visual Aids: Utilize diagrams, charts, and mind maps to visualize intricate concepts. Visual aids facilitate comprehension and memory recall.Peer Collaboration: Collaborate with peers for group discussions, study sessions, and peer teaching.

Explaining concepts to others reinforces your understanding and offers alternate viewpoints.

Mindfulness and Stress Management:

- Practice Mindfulness: Engage in mindfulness techniques such as meditation and deep breathing to alleviate stress and enhance concentration. Mindfulness nurtures cognitive function and emotional regulation.
- Breaks and Rest: Integrate short breaks into your study routine to prevent burnout. A refreshed mind is more receptive to learning and effective problem-solving.
- Healthy Lifestyle: Maintain a balanced diet, regular exercise, and sufficient sleep. A healthy lifestyle supports cognitive function and overall well-being.

Seek Support and Resources:

- Utilize Educator Support: Reach out to teachers or professors for clarifications on challenging topics. Educators can offer guidance, supplemental resources, or alternative explanations.
- Academic Support Centers: Many educational institutions offer academic support centers providing tutoring, workshops, and resources to assist in overcoming challenges.
- Online Resources: Capitalize on online platforms, educational websites, and videos for supplementary learning materials. Online resources provide diverse perspectives and explanations.

Embrace Failure and Adapt:

- Learn from Mistakes: Instead of fearing failure, view it as a catalyst for growth. Analyze your errors, comprehend their underlying causes, and adjust your approach for enhancement.
- Adapt Strategies: Should a study technique or approach yield subpar results, be open to experimentation. Adaptability is pivotal in discovering methods aligned with your learning style and requirements.

Foster a Supportive Environment:

- Positive Peer Relationships: Surround yourself with supportive and optimistic peers. Encourage one another, exchange insights, and offer assistance when required.
- Family Support: Communicate with your family about your learning challenges and aspirations. Their encouragement, understanding, and support significantly contribute to your triumphs.
- Stay Organized: Maintain an organized study space free from distractions. A clutter-free environment fosters concentration and productivity.

By employing these strategies, students can navigate obstacles with self-assurance and emerge as more capable individuals. Ultimately, overcoming these challenges will build self-confidence in students. Building that grit is crucial to their personal, academic, and future professional success. A strong sense of self-assurance empowers students to tackle challenges, engage actively in learning, and confidently navigate social interactions.

Self-confidence serves as the foundation upon which students build their abilities and accomplishments. They are more likely to seek new knowledge and skills throughout their lives, leading to continuous personal and professional growth. Self-confidence is a crucial attribute of influential leaders. Students who develop self-confidence are better prepared to take on leadership roles and inspire others.

Students who believe in their abilities are likely to engage actively in their learning process. They approach assignments and exams positively, leading to better performance. Students with higher levels of self-confidence are more likely to participate in classroom discussions, share their ideas, and seek help when needed, which enhances their understanding of the subject matter.

Confident students are better communicators. They can express their ideas clearly and persuasively, which is essential in academic and professional contexts. Similarly, a healthy level of self-confidence also enhances students' ability to establish and maintain positive relationships. They are more likely to engage in healthy interactions and assert their boundaries.

A healthy level of self-confidence contributes to a positive self-image. Students who feel good about themselves are more likely to have a realistic perspective of their strengths and weaknesses. This self-awareness enables them to set achievable goals and work toward self-improvement.

Self-confidence encourages students to step out of their comfort zones and take calculated risks. Students who believe in their abilities are more likely to experiment, innovate, and explore new ideas. This mindset is essential for personal and intellectual growth.

Confident students are better equipped to cope with challenges and setbacks. They view failures as opportunities for learning and growth rather than as indicators of their worth. This resilience is crucial for developing a healthy attitude toward setbacks and disappointments.

Strategies for Cultivating Student Self-Confidence:

Fostering self-confidence in students requires a holistic approach involving educators, parents, and students. Educators can use these ffective strategies that can contribute to building and nurturing student self-confidence:

Encourage Positive Self-Talk: Help students recognize their inner dialogue and replace self-doubt with positive affirmations. Encourage them to identify their strengths and accomplishments, reinforcing their self-belief.

Set Realistic Goals: Assist students in setting achievable goals that align with their abilities and interests. Celebrate their progress toward these goals to boost their sense of accomplishment and confidence.

Provide Constructive Feedback: Offer specific and constructive feedback that highlights students' strengths and areas for improvement. This helps students understand where they excel and what aspects they can work on without feeling discouraged.

Embrace Mistakes as Learning Opportunities: Teach students to view mistakes as stepping stones to improvement rather than as failures. Discuss the importance of learning from mistakes and trying again, which builds resilience and confidence.

Encourage Participation: Create a supportive classroom environment where students feel comfortable sharing their thoughts and ideas. Encourage participation in discussions, group activities, and presentations to boost their confidence in expressing themselves.

Offer Choices: Empower students by allowing them to make decisions about their learning. When students have a say in their education, they feel a sense of ownership and control, contributing to their confidence.

Celebrate Diversity: Highlight the uniqueness of each student and emphasize that everyone has strengths and talents. Create an atmosphere that celebrates diversity and helps students recognize their contributions.

Model Self-Confidence: Educators and parents can model self-confidence in their behavior and interactions. When students observe adults who believe in themselves and confidently handle challenges, they are more likely to adopt similar attitudes.

A strong sense of self-confidence empowers students to excel academically, navigate challenges, and thrive in various aspects of life. Educators and parents can nurture students' self-confidence by implementing strategies that promote positive self-talk, goal-setting, and resilience. The benefits of self-confidence extend far beyond the classroom, shaping students into resilient, capable individuals who are well-prepared to achieve their goals and contribute positively to society. As students develop their self-confidence, they embark on self-discovery and growth that will serve them well.

"Student choice in what and how they are showing academic success is important to learning. In their real world, our students will be tasked with the challenges of sharing information with others. Whether that be in a job for a presentation or in a club when sharing outcomes with others."

Stevie Frank
Technology Coach/Education Consultant
@StevieFrank23

Chapter 9

Nurturing Leadership Skills in Students
A Path to Empowerment

Leadership skills have become essential for students to thrive in various spheres of life. Beyond traditional notions of authority, leadership encompasses communication, empathy, and problem-solving qualities that contribute to personal growth and collective progress. Nurturing these skills in students prepares them for future roles and equips them with the tools to make a positive impact. Let's explore how educators and mentors can foster leadership skills in students, paving the way for a brighter future.

Leadership is best cultivated when students are presented with stories and narratives of individuals who have exemplified exceptional leadership. These stories inspire students and offer relatable examples of how leadership can manifest across various backgrounds and circumstances. Educators can ignite students' interest and curiosity about leadership's potential by sharing stories of leaders from diverse fields—from historical figures to contemporary change-makers.

Authentic leadership begins with the ability to think critically and independently. Encouraging students to question assumptions, challenge norms, and explore different perspectives lays the foundation for innovative thinking. Teachers can facilitate discussions promoting open-mindedness and guiding students to analyze complex issues from multiple angles. This approach not only fosters intellectual growth but also nurtures the qualities of adaptability and creative problem-solving.

Influential leaders are adept communicators who can articulate their ideas clearly and persuasively. Educators can integrate activities that promote communication skills in the classroom, such as debates, group discussions, and presentations. Providing a platform for students to express their thoughts and engage in constructive dialogues enhances their ability to convey ideas and boosts their self-confidence.

Developing leadership skills begins with understanding oneself. Encouraging students to reflect on their strengths, weaknesses, and values helps them cultivate self-awareness—a cornerstone of effective leadership. By guiding students through reflective exercises, mentors can help them discover their unique leadership styles and harness their potential to lead authentically.

Leadership is not a solitary endeavor; it involves collaboration and empathy. Creating collaborative projects that require students to work together, communicate, and understand differing viewpoints can foster a sense of unity and cooperation. Through these experiences, students develop empathy by considering the feelings and perspectives of their peers, an invaluable trait for effective leadership.

Leadership often emerges in the face of challenges. Introducing students to real-world problems—locally or globally—allows them to apply their skills to find innovative solutions. By working on these issues, students develop confidence in their ability to effect positive change and recognize their capacity to lead in impactful ways.

Empowering students to take initiative and assume responsibility for their actions is pivotal to leadership development. Cultivate them to identify areas for improvement, propose solutions, and take the lead in implementing these changes. By embracing responsibility, students learn accountability and experience the satisfaction of seeing their efforts translate into positive outcomes.

Mentorship plays a significant role in leadership development. Establishing mentor-mentee relationships connects students with experienced individuals who can offer guidance, share insights, and provide constructive feedback. Mentors can help students navigate challenges, set goals, and refine their leadership skills through personalized support.

Integrating discussions about ethics and values into leadership development is crucial. Prompt students to consider the moral implications of their decisions and actions as leaders. By understanding the ethical dimensions of leadership, students learn to make responsible choices that align with their values.

Leadership often involves navigating uncertainties and setbacks. Teaching students to embrace failure as a stepping stone to growth and encouraging them to persevere in facing challenges nurtures resilience. Adapting to changing circumstances equips students with the flexibility to lead effectively in an ever-evolving world.

So how can we take that theory and need of leadership and create and promote "ways" students can lead in the school, class, and community?

Here are ways students **can be leaders in a school** building. These roles empower students to create a positive, supportive, and engaging school environment for everyone.

- **Peer Mentoring:** Students can volunteer to mentor younger or less experienced students, offering academic, social, or emotional support.
- **Student Council:** Participating in the student council allows students to voice their opinions, plan events, and advocate for their peers' needs and concerns.
- **Club or Organization Leadership:** Taking on leadership roles in school clubs or organizations allows students to organize activities, manage budgets, and create a positive impact within a specific interest group.
- **Tutoring:** Students can offer their expertise to tutor classmates who need help in specific

subjects, fostering a collaborative learning environment.
- **Community Service Initiatives:** Organizing and leading school-based community service projects, such as fundraisers, clean-up campaigns, or charity drives, demonstrates leadership while giving back to the community.
- **Event Planning:** Students can lead the planning and execution of school events like dances, fundraisers, or talent shows, showcasing their organizational and teamwork skills.
- **Environmental Stewardship:** Taking the lead in implementing eco-friendly initiatives, such as recycling programs or awareness campaigns, highlights a student's environmental commitment.
- **Conflict Resolution:** Students can act as mediators or peer counselors to help resolve conflicts among classmates, promoting a harmonious and inclusive school environment.
- **Tech and Media Leadership:** Managing the school's social media accounts, creating digital content, or assisting with technology-related issues positions students as leaders in the digital realm.
- **Inclusion Advocacy:** Students can lead efforts to promote diversity and inclusion by organizing cultural awareness events, workshops, or discussions that celebrate differences and foster understanding.

Additionally, students **can be leaders in a classroom.** These roles empower students to develop leadership skills and promote a positive classroom atmosphere.

- **Classroom Assistant:** Students can take turns being the classroom helper, assisting the teacher with tasks like distributing materials, organizing supplies, or setting up activities.
- **Peer Tutoring:** Students can offer to help their classmates understand challenging concepts, providing academic support and fostering a collaborative learning atmosphere.
- **Group Facilitator:** Students can lead group activities or discussions, ensuring everyone's voice is heard and the group stays on track.
- **Presentation Leader:** Encourage students to present projects or reports to the class, helping to enhance their public speaking and organizational skills.
- **Tech Expert:** Tech-savvy students can assist their peers with using digital tools, troubleshooting technical issues or explaining how to navigate online platforms.
- **Inclusion Ambassador:** Students can actively promote inclusivity by ensuring everyone feels welcome, engaging shy or new classmates, and preventing exclusion.
- **Morning Meeting Leader:** Assign students the role of leading the class during morning meetings, helping to set a positive tone for the day and fostering a sense of community.

- **Classroom Librarian:** Students can manage the classroom library, recommending books, keeping it organized, and creating a welcoming reading environment.
- **Timekeeper:** Designate a student to help manage time during activities, reminding the class about task transitions or time limits.
- **Classroom Decorator:** Allow students to take responsibility for decorating bulletin boards or creating displays that showcase the class's achievements and learning progress.

School and classrooms are not the only places students can show leadership. Being **community leaders** can have a lasting impact on their personal growth and sense of civic responsibility.

- **Community Service Projects:** Organize or participate in community volunteer projects that address local needs, such as food drives, park clean-ups, or assisting at local shelters.
- **Youth Advisory Boards:** Join or establish youth advisory boards to provide input and insights on community issues and policies, representing the voice of young residents.
- **Environmental Initiatives:** Lead initiatives to promote sustainability, such as tree planting, recycling programs, or awareness campaigns about conservation practices.
- **Health and Wellness Advocacy:** Create campaigns to raise awareness about healthy lifestyles, mental health, or wellness practices

and organize events encouraging community members to adopt healthier habits.
- **Cultural and Diversity Events:** Organize cultural fairs, workshops, or events that celebrate the diversity within the community, fostering understanding and unity among different groups.
- **Senior Citizen Outreach:** Initiate programs to connect with and assist elderly community members, offering companionship, food assistance, or technology help for seniors.
- **Community Garden or Green Spaces:** Lead efforts to establish community gardens or maintain green spaces, providing residents opportunities to grow their produce and enjoy outdoor areas.
- **Educational Workshops:** Organize workshops on financial literacy, resume writing, or digital skills, helping community members acquire valuable knowledge.
- **Neighborhood Safety Campaigns:** Lead campaigns focusing on neighborhood safety, such as organizing crime prevention seminars, setting up neighborhood watch programs, or promoting pedestrian safety.
- **Art and Culture Projects:** Spearhead public art installations, murals, or cultural performances that enhance the community's aesthetics and promote artistic expression.

Cultivating leadership skills in students is a holistic endeavor that goes beyond a mere checklist of attributes. It involves fostering a mindset of empowerment, curiosity, and empathy. Educators and mentors can guide students on a transformative journey of self-discovery and personal growth by creating an environment that encourages independent thinking, effective communication, collaboration, and ethical decision-making. Nurturing these skills equips students with the tools they need to lead and contribute positively to their communities and impact the world.

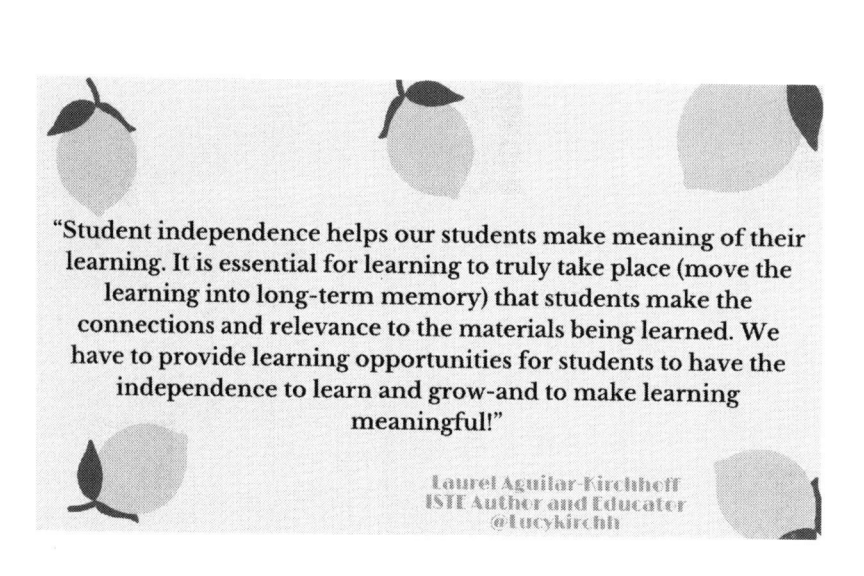

"Student independence helps our students make meaning of their learning. It is essential for learning to truly take place (move the learning into long-term memory) that students make the connections and relevance to the materials being learned. We have to provide learning opportunities for students to have the independence to learn and grow-and to make learning meaningful!"

Laurel Aguilar-Kirchhoff
ISTE Author and Educator
@Lucykirchh

Chapter 10

Moving from Consumption to Student Creation

In today's rapidly growing world, where information is just a few clicks away, traditional modes of education are being challenged. The shift from passive student consumption of knowledge to active student creation has become an essential pedagogical approach. This transition empowers students to take charge of their learning and fosters creativity, critical thinking, and problem-solving skills that are vital for success in the 21st century.

The digital age has democratized information access, breaking down barriers to knowledge acquisition. The internet offers a vast repository of resources, enabling students to acquire information from multiple sources and formats. As a result, the role of educators is no longer confined to mere dispensers of knowledge. Instead, they are tasked with effectively guiding students in navigating this information landscape.

Educational institutions are increasingly recognizing the limitations of a curriculum centered solely around rote learning and passive consumption. Modern educators need to equip students with the skills required to analyze, synthesize, and apply knowledge in real-world scenarios. Consequently, a paradigm shift towards student creation is gaining traction.

The Essence of Student Creation

Student creation in education encompasses many activities that encourage active engagement and originality. These activities include writing original essays, designing experiments, developing software, composing music, creating artwork, producing videos, and even conceptualizing entrepreneurial ventures. The common thread among these endeavors is that they require students to move beyond the role of information recipients to that of creators and contributors.

By engaging in creative endeavors, students deepen their understanding of a subject and develop a unique perspective that enriches their learning experience. Creation demands a higher level of cognitive engagement involving critical thinking, problem-solving, decision-making, and applying theoretical concepts to practical contexts. This process transforms students into active participants in their education, fostering a sense of ownership and responsibility.

Creativity and critical thinking are indispensable in today's rapidly changing world. Traditional education often emphasizes convergent thinking, where there is a single correct answer, rather than divergent thinking, which involves generating multiple solutions to a problem. Student creation promotes divergent thinking by encouraging students to explore various avenues, experiment with ideas, and develop innovative solutions.

Moreover, through creation, students encounter challenges and setbacks, which necessitate critical thinking to overcome. They learn to evaluate their work critically, identify areas for improvement, and iterate upon their creations. This iterative process mirrors real-world scenarios where solutions are rarely perfect on the first attempt. By experiencing this creation, evaluation, and improvement cycle, students develop resilience and an intrinsic motivation to learn.

The shift from consumption to creation aligns closely with the concept of a growth mindset, popularized by psychologist Carol Dweck. A growth mindset emphasizes the belief that abilities and intelligence can be developed through dedication, hard work, and continuous learning. When students engage in creation, they are more likely to adopt a growth mindset as they experience firsthand the connection between effort, improvement, and achievement.

In a consumption-oriented education system, students might develop a fixed mindset, assuming their abilities are static and unchangeable. However, when they become creators, they see their capabilities as malleable. Challenges are seen as opportunities for growth rather than insurmountable barriers. This shift in perspective enhances their academic performance and equips them with a positive outlook on life's challenges.

Transitioning from a consumption-based model to one that promotes creation is challenging. Educators, students, and even parents might resist this change due to concerns about the perceived additional workload, unfamiliarity with new tools and methods, and potential risks of failure. Addressing these concerns and highlighting the long-term benefits of fostering creativity, critical thinking, and a growth mindset is crucial.

Professional development for educators is essential to ensure they are well-equipped to guide students in their creative pursuits. Incorporating technology and digital tools that facilitate creation can ease the transition. Providing a supportive environment where failure is reframed as a valuable learning experience can alleviate fears of risk-taking and failure.

Implementing Student Creation in Education

To facilitate the shift from student consumption to student creation, educational institutions can consider several strategies:

- **Project-Based Learning:** Integrate project-based learning into the curriculum, where students work on real-world projects that require them to apply knowledge to solve complex problems.
- **Collaborative Activities:** Encourage collaborative activities that involve brainstorming, peer review, and teamwork,

fostering diverse perspectives and creative synergies.
- **Assessment Redesign:** Rethink assessment methods to include more open-ended questions, projects, and presentations that require students to demonstrate not just knowledge but also their ability to create and communicate effectively.
- **Incorporate Technology:** Utilize technology tools that enable students to create digital content, interactive presentations, and multimedia projects that go beyond traditional written assignments.
- **Teacher as Facilitator:** Shift the role of the teacher from a lecturer to a facilitator who guides and supports students in their creative endeavors.
- **Cultivate Curiosity:** Foster a classroom culture that values curiosity and inquiry, encouraging students to ask questions and explore topics that genuinely interest them.

The transformation from student consumption to student creation represents a fundamental shift in the educational landscape. It is a shift that embraces the complexities of the digital age while nurturing timeless skills of creativity, critical thinking, and adaptability. As educators, parents, and society recognize the need for holistic development, the movement toward student creation gathers momentum.

By embracing this change, educational institutions can equip students with the tools they need to thrive in an ever-changing world. A generation of creators, innovators, and problem solvers will emerge, armed with the confidence to tackle challenges, the resilience to overcome setbacks, and the vision to shape a better future. The journey from passive consumers to active creators is not just an educational evolution; it's a societal revolution that holds the promise of a brighter tomorrow.

Project ideas that I have tried as a teacher and school and district leader that students can complete to showcase their learning across various subjects and disciplines:

- **Research Paper or Presentation:** Students can choose a topic of interest, conduct research, and present their findings through a well-structured paper or presentation.
- **Creative Writing Piece:** This could be a short story, poem, play, or even a novel chapter, demonstrating their understanding of literary elements and storytelling techniques.
- **Science Experiment:** Students can design and conduct an experiment, record observations, analyze data, and present their conclusions and any unexpected results.
- **Historical Reenactment or Simulation:** Students can recreate a historical event, era, or figure through reenactments, role-playing, or digital simulations.
- **Art Portfolio:** Showcase different art techniques, styles, and concepts through a collection of visual artworks accompanied by explanations of their artistic choices.

- **Mathematical Modeling Project:** Students can apply mathematical concepts to real-world problems, creating models and simulations to demonstrate their understanding.
- **Language Learning Podcast:** Students can record a series of podcasts in a foreign language they're learning, discussing topics and engaging in conversations.
- **Community Service Project:** Design and execute a project that addresses a community issue, such as organizing a clean-up drive, a charity event, or a workshop.
- **Digital Media Presentation:** Create a multimedia presentation incorporating images, videos, audio, and interactive elements to convey complex concepts.
- **Business Plan or Entrepreneurial Pitch:** Develop a business idea, create a business plan, and pitch it as if presenting to potential investors.
- **Cultural Exhibition:** Research and curate an exhibition about a specific culture, including artifacts, traditions, and historical context.
- **Environmental Sustainability Campaign:** Create a campaign to raise awareness about environmental issues and propose actionable steps for sustainability.
- **Music Composition:** Compose an original piece of music that showcases their understanding of musical theory, harmony, and melody.
- **Engineering Design Challenge:** Design and build a prototype of a device or structure that addresses a real-world engineering problem.

- **Health and Fitness Plan:** Create a comprehensive health and fitness plan, incorporating research on nutrition, exercise routines, and overall well-being.
- **Debate or Mock Trial:** Engage in a debate or mock trial to demonstrate their understanding of legal concepts, research, and persuasive communication.
- **Documentary Film:** Produce a documentary on a historical event, social issue, or scientific discovery, combining research, interviews, and visuals.
- **Philanthropy Project:** Develop a project that involves fundraising, donation drives, or volunteering for a charitable cause.
- **Virtual Reality Tour:** Create a virtual reality tour of a historical site, museum, or fictional world, incorporating interactive elements and informative narration.

These projects encourage students to delve deep into their subject matter, apply critical thinking, problem-solving skills, and creativity, and showcase their learning in innovative and meaningful ways.

Hands-on Learning

Student creation pairs well with hands-on learning, also known as experiential learning. Hands-on learning is an educational approach that emphasizes active engagement with the subject matter through direct experience and interaction. This method involves students actively participating in activities that require them to manipulate objects, perform experiments, solve problems, and engage in real-world scenarios. Hands-on learning holds several key benefits for students:

- **Active Engagement:** Hands-on learning keeps students actively engaged in the learning process. This engagement is crucial for maintaining their attention, interest, and motivation, which can lead to deeper understanding and retention of information.
- **Concrete Understanding:** When students physically interact with objects or perform tasks, they develop a concrete understanding of abstract concepts. This helps bridge the gap between theory and practice, making complex ideas more accessible.
- **Critical Thinking:** Hands-on activities often require students to analyze, synthesize, and apply knowledge to real situations. This encourages the development of critical thinking skills as students navigate challenges, make decisions, and solve problems.
- **Long-Term Retention:** Active participation in learning activities enhances memory retention. When students experience concepts firsthand, they create meaningful connections that are more likely to stay with them over time.
- **Personal Relevance:** Hands-on learning allows students to connect classroom learning to their own lives and experiences. This personal relevance can increase their interest and enthusiasm for the subject matter.

- **Skill Development:** Many hands-on activities require students to develop practical skills, such as observation, experimentation, communication, teamwork, and problem-solving. These skills are transferable to various contexts and are valuable for lifelong learning.
- **Reduced Fear of Failure:** Hands-on learning environments often encourage experimentation and risk-taking. Students learn that failure is a natural part of the learning process and can lead to growth and improvement.
- **Collaboration:** Many hands-on activities involve collaboration and teamwork. Students learn to communicate effectively, share ideas, and work together to achieve a common goal.
- **Real-World Application:** Hands-on learning helps students see the practical applications of their learning. This can motivate them by demonstrating the relevance of their education to their future careers and everyday lives.
- **Intrinsic Motivation:** Experiencing the satisfaction of completing a hands-on task successfully can lead to intrinsic motivation, where a sense of accomplishment and curiosity drives students.
- **Cultural and Emotional Understanding:** Hands-on activities can help students gain insights into different cultures, historical periods, and perspectives. It can also foster empathy and emotional understanding through immersive experiences.

Incorporating hands-on learning into education requires a shift from passive consumption to active participation. It encourages educators to create dynamic and interactive learning environments that accommodate a variety of learning styles. By providing students with opportunities to explore, experiment, and discover, hands-on learning promotes holistic development, fostering academic growth and the skills and qualities needed for success in an ever-evolving world. The transition from passive learners to active participants marks a paradigm shift that aligns education with the needs of the modern world. It empowers students to become adaptable, innovative thinkers who can thrive in a rapidly changing landscape. By fostering active participation, educators create an environment that not only imparts knowledge but also nurtures the skills and mindset required for success and fulfillment in the 21st century.

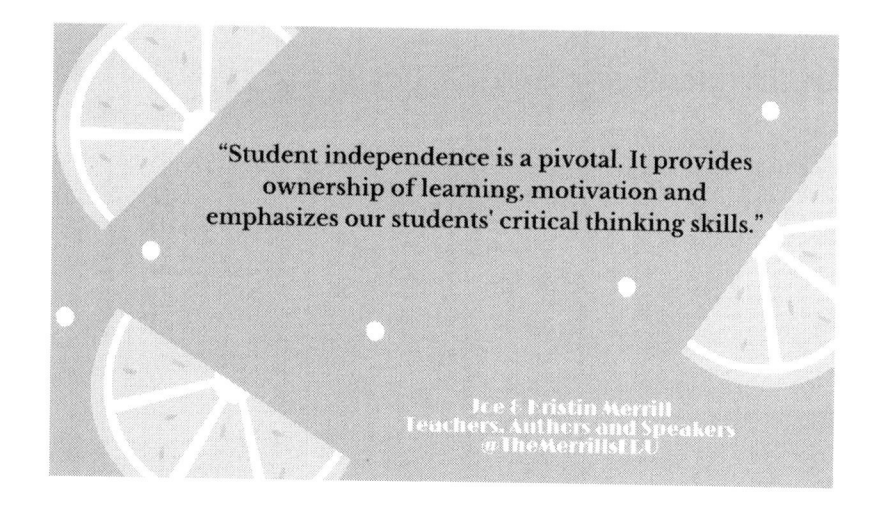

"Student independence is a pivotal. It provides ownership of learning, motivation and emphasizes our students' critical thinking skills."

Joe & Kristin Merrill
Teachers, Authors and Speakers
@TheMerrillsEDU

Chapter 11

Students as Creators of Content

By Laurie Guyon

Children are innately curious. When talking with adults, they ask the why, what, and how questions. They also stare at things that catch their attention and touch and feel as they explore. Give a child a new toy, and they inevitably will play with the box it came in. Nothing is more exciting to a child than a blank canvas that they get to make their own. They find potential in whatever they see around them. Take a child hiking in the woods, and they will collect sticks, leaves, insects, and rocks along the way. Stop for a bit, and they are designing fairy houses, having a stick sword fight, or watching a bug crawl along a leaf. Spend a day with a child on a driveway with some chalk, and they will create roads, simple games, and all sorts of designs. Everything around them has potential. Everything offers opportunity.

But somewhere in their schooling, this curiosity gets kiboshed. While I have shifted from the classroom into an administrative role, I still spend about a third of the school year in classrooms. I am walking the halls of schools almost daily. I am fortunate to be an observer, a coach, and a cheerleader of all that teachers do daily to help their students learn. I've observed that students become less curious between second and third grade. They get accustomed to school rules and become compliant. Just watch a kindergarten class walk down the hall. A handful follow the teacher's directions and walk in a straight line, a few students are giggling and causing gaps they can then run to close, and others are touching everything they can and waving to you as you pass by. Still, others are observing their surroundings and are oblivious that the line is moving. Observe a third grade class, and the number who are following the rules has increased significantly.

The same is true in our traditional classroom design. I push into classes to teach digital citizenship, computer science, and how to use technology tools. When I am in the K-2 grades, I often let students do free exploration first before I give much direction. They are incredible thinkers, observers, and button pushers. Students are not afraid of doing something wrong. Instead, they ask excellent questions, help each other, and find joy when they are successful. By third grade, however, students raise their hands more and ask what to do next instead of trying it out for themselves. But we need them to stay curious. We need our students to be creators. We need innovators and independent thinkers. Our world demands these skills and requires us to encourage curiosity.

Creators can come up with new ideas and solutions to problems. They are not afraid of failure but look at it as part of the iterative process. What stops us from supporting student creation? Is it time? Is it a lack of interest? Do we need to figure out how to encourage it? Are we tied to a scripted curriculum that doesn't allow for much creation? Look at your practice and consider how often you have students create. I mean really create, not just completing an activity for a holiday that has every student making the same thing. I am talking about stepping aside and letting your student's imaginations soar.

Why? Because we want independent, confident, and resilient innovators who will push to improve the world. Students who have a champion for them will be more likely to develop these critical skills.

- Independent thinkers can analyze situations and make their own decisions.
- Confident students are open to challenge authority and question the status quo.
- Resiliency helps students stand up for what they believe in.
- Innovators can take new ideas and turn them into reality.
- Investigators can see the potential in new ideas and make them happen.

It's up to us to encourage students to think for themselves. We can challenge them to come up with solutions to problems and give them the chance to be the drivers of their learning. We can encourage students to think about how they might start their businesses or develop new technologies. Help your students learn about the world while immersing themselves in it.

All of these skills are essential for meeting and exceeding success. The world is changing rapidly, and the only way to keep up is to think creatively and solve problems. Students who are creators, independent thinkers, and innovators will be well-prepared for future challenges.

Whether you are just starting the year off with a new set of students or you are knee-deep in the trenches, you can do some simple things to empower students toward their academic and skill achievement. These may seem simple, but they can have so many positive outcomes. Let's start with the nonnegotiables of building a classroom that empowers student success.

Empowerment Tip #1: Greet your students every day.

I am talking about getting out of your classroom, standing in the hallway, and greeting your students as they enter your classroom—every day. Every day is an opportunity to build trust, establish routines, and show you care about your students. I'm sure you have seen on social media teachers who have handshakes or dance moves for each student. While that's all great, you don't have to go that far. A simple smile and acknowledgment that you are happy they are here is all you need. If you want to do the dance or the handshakes, go for it! But make sure it's genuine and that you are doing it because you and your students are on board with it.

Students as Creators of Content

Studies have shown how important it is to greet your students at the door. One study by the Journal of Positive Behavior Interventions noted that this simple routine can improve academic achievement by 20% and decrease disruptive behavior by 9%. It builds a community in your classroom, enabling students to feel safe and valued in everything they do.

If you cannot be at the door each day, you can offer other ways to tell them they are welcome. When I taught 6th grade, I bought a small whiteboard at the dollar store. I hung it outside my classroom so that if I could not be there, I could at least have some way to greet them. Every day, I put a quote, a silly fact, or a saying on it. During the first week of school, I often had some students think it was funny to run their fingers through it and make it difficult to read. But by the end of that first week, students started to look forward to what it said, and it was never tampered with again.

I always kept the whiteboard greetings positive and offered students something they could remember or use. There were a few favorites over the years:

'THROW KINDNESS AROUND LIKE CONFETTI"

"WHEN SOMETHING GOES WRONG IN YOUR LIFE, JUST YELL, 'PLOT TWIST!' AND MOVE ON"

"THERE IS NO ANGRY WAY TO SAY BUBBLES"

Students would read the quotes and then come into the room and repeat them. For the bubbles one, they would try to say the word as angry as they can at each other. They would often repeat the word bubbles when feeling tense to break any tension. Sometimes, I'd tie the quote into something we were doing. For example, I used the plot twist quote when rewriting the endings of classic stories. It helped set the stage for the lesson.

More often than not, the quotes were there to make them smile. It was a way to reset as they came in the door and got them ready for my class. I tried to make it to the door every day, but if something took me away from that spot, I knew I still greeted them. I found even other educators enjoyed stopping and reading the quote of the day after I was out for a day. They said they missed my daily positivity. I started leaving quotes for my substitutes to put on the board so that it changed daily.

Again, this was a simple way to build community. But the payoff was huge. Adding something simple like this to your daily routines will help cultivate the mindset that your classroom is a safe place and a place to spread joy.

Empowerment Tip #2: Breathe

Recently, I was in a classroom with a sign above the door. It said 'Just Breathe.' I asked the teacher about it, and he stated that when students enter the classroom, they are encouraged to take a deep breath and release any tension or stress. It's a clear physical reset that can have incredible outcomes. The research on breathing techniques for lowering stress, calming nerves, and decreasing anxiety proves that this simple routine can benefit students.

Think about the amount of stress you feel every day. Now imagine the daily stress your students experience, especially considering they don't always know how to handle it. Teaching your students simple breathing techniques can help them manage their daily stress.

I use breathing techniques often when I push into classrooms. We use them as 'brain breaks' embedded in the lessons. But they don't have to be used that way. If you are teaching a lesson on computational thinking, you can use a breathing algorithm like five finger or box breathing. You can use breathing techniques to engage your students in a science lesson or have them think before they speak in a Socratic seminar.

I was once asked to push into a universal pre-K classroom to teach the foundations of digital citizenship. I was scheduled to come for the last half hour of the school day. When I entered the classroom, the teacher did a math lesson on her Promethean board. No student in the class sat in their chair the right way, and everyone looked exhausted. The teacher saw me come in and gave me that 'good luck' smile, and went to sit down. I could tell I needed to do something before starting the lesson to refocus the students. I decided to do a quick five-finger breathing with the students. By the time we finished the first hand, I could see their shoulders lower, they were sitting more still, and they were able to focus. On the other hand, they were ready to learn.

I could have just as quickly done a wiggle type break, but this one added focus and started to build that community as I encouraged them through the simple routine. If you can take your students outside to do these types of activities, even better! Fresh air, movement, and simple breathing techniques go a long way toward building student empowerment.

Empowerment Tip #3: Affirmations

In school, we often focus on what students need to learn. We identify what they did wrong and think of strategies to help them. When we sit with a student and review a math sheet or an essay, we often point out areas of improvement or where they went wrong on a problem. While it is essential to help our students learn, we also need to show them their strengths and help them identify what it is they have inside them.

Positivity can go a long way toward helping our students be empowered. A few great techniques that take almost no time at all will build resilience and confidence in your students. Here is your homework. Watch the TED talk by Amy Cuddy: Your body language may shape who you are.

Practice your power pose often and teach it to your students. Then, take it further and get your students to say positive things about themselves. Do this often.

When I was in high school, I took a leadership class. It was an honor to be included in the class, as your teachers nominated you to be a part of it. I loved this class. Every day, we focused on what we can do. It didn't have grades or require the same tasks we often do in regular classes. Instead, we were given opportunities to be leaders. This included service work and was all project-based learning. I thrived in it.

Looking back at why that class helped me be more confident, I realize it was because the teacher focused on what we COULD do versus what we SHOULD do. She opened doors and had us focus on what we did well. She did an exercise that allowed us to share the strengths we saw in others. She had us write one positive thing about each student in the class on lined paper. We then had to cut those things out and place them into the paper bags on our desk. We were prohibited from reading what others wrote about us until we went home. I remember sitting on my bed and reaching into my paper bag. I was so nervous about what others would say about me. This was an activity that was unchecked by the teacher, so the strips could say anything. But as I pulled out the papers individually, I saw trends in what people saw in me. My peers saw me as friendly, positive, smiley, and inclusive. I cried. I hadn't realized how much I needed to hear positive feedback and realized how little I valued those skills in myself. But, if others recognized them as my strengths, I realized they are my gifts.

Affirmations can help your students realize their gifts and build confidence in them. They are things you say about yourself that you repeat often. Celebrities use them. Leaders use them. And you can teach your students to use them too. If you need help figuring out how to start, check out YouTube for some simple videos to follow, or do a Google search to find some. If you are on TikTok, search the term affirmations to learn some for yourself, too!

Utilizing these three simple empowerment tips will foster a community in your classroom. It will be a class where your students feel valued and it will help them realize and focus on their strengths. From there, we can then foster that curiosity and wonder. Offer opportunities for students to find out information on their own. Yes, you have a curriculum your students must get through, but there is more than one way for them to learn it. And if it's student-driven, the learning will be deeper and longer lasting.

You want to build intrinsic as well as extrinsic motivation. The time it takes to allow free exploration doesn't need to be long. In fact, I encourage you to give parameters. We all know that our students can scroll through TikTok for hours. Instead, we want targeted exploration. Give time constraints that are feasible for you and for them to start. For example, ask students what they know about a topic and then ask them to learn three things about it before diving in. Give them time to explore. For your younger students, use school-approved sites like Pebble Go, Wonderopolis.org, or whatever you have available for them. For older students, help them narrow a search on Google to get the information they want.

Then, have them share what they learned. Allow your students to talk to each other. Encourage eye contact and encourage them to dig deeper into their research if they have more questions. Finally, have them share the top three things they learned as a group. Now, you can cover any content you need because they are all in and ready to learn.

This type of learning doesn't take much time, but the payoffs are enormous. You are then fostering that curiosity. You are encouraging problem-solving. You are helping to keep your students engaged in their learning. Getting your students to see the strengths in themselves will always be a win. Students should have opportunities to create and drive their knowledge often. Let your students lead the way and watch the possibilities and their potential shine.

Laurie Guyon (@SMILELearning) is the Lead Coordinator for Instructional Technology Programs at WSWHE BOCES in Saratoga Springs, New York. She is the Capital Region Director and a trainer for The New York State Association for Computers and Technologies in Education (NYSCATE). Laurie is also an adjunct professor for SUNY Plattsburgh, where she teaches Digital Age Learning in the CAS SBL program. She is the author of SMILE Learning: Leveraging the Power of Educational Technology.

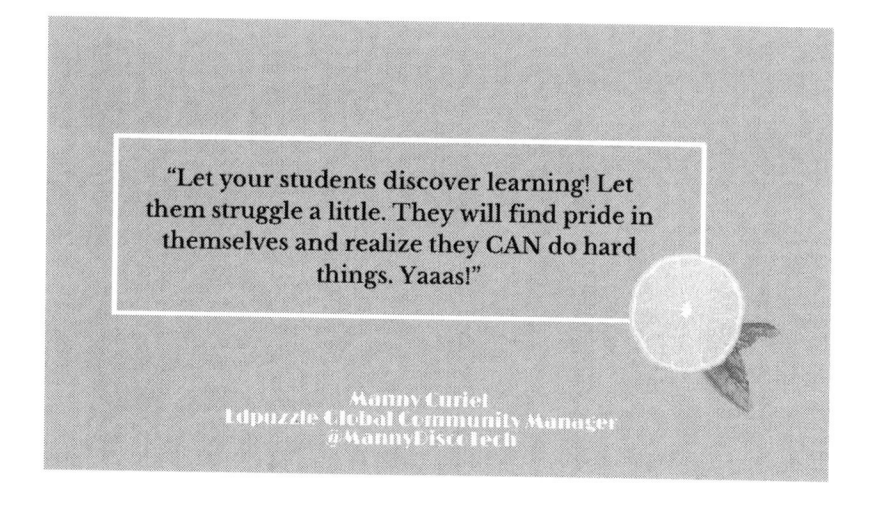

"Let your students discover learning! Let them struggle a little. They will find pride in themselves and realize they CAN do hard things. Yaaas!"

Manny Curiel
Edpuzzle Global Community Manager
@MannyDiscoTech

Chapter 12

Creating Lemonade Stand Moments for All Learners

By Dr. Marialice B.F.X. Curran

My Journey

Panic sets in as I begin to count how many paragraphs and how many rows of students are ahead of me. I count down to my paragraph and start practicing my part over and over in my head. I hear absolutely nothing else until the teacher calls my name to read next. With some apprehension in my voice, I begin to read until I'm interrupted by the teacher who tells me that I'm reading the wrong paragraph. The class bursts into laughter as I quickly turn the shame I feel into a comedy routine and I shrug my shoulders and laugh as if I planned it this way.

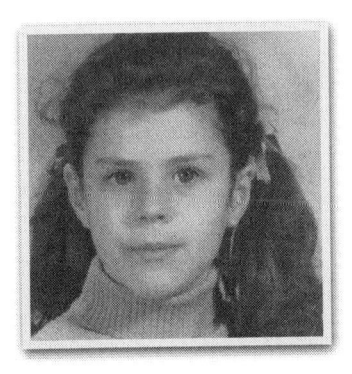

Young school picture of Marialice with brunette pigtails with
little blue bows matching the light blue turtleneck

This exact scenario continued to happen year after year throughout my K-12 school experience. I learned how to perfect being the class clown early in life as a way to protect myself from the embarrassment I carried for not being able to learn like everyone else. By the time I was in the third grade, my parents were called into school and they were told I was the R word. They sought outside testing which led to a diagnosis of dyslexia. That label haunted me as the majority of my teachers never took the time to understand me as a learner.

Although I was an absolute failure in a traditional classroom and I could easily recount all the ways school failed me, I have always made the conscious decision to focus on the handful of grown-ups in school who chose to see something extraordinary in me instead of just the label. Mrs. Lane, Mr. McGrath, Mrs. Cronin, Mr. Mac (my soccer coach), Mrs. Howard, Mr. Tracy, and my student teacher in Latin I that I had to repeat twice, Ms. Loeb. Each of them took the time to stop at my lemonade stand and bring out the very best in me. Without them, I would have believed I was just the label and that owning the class clown role was the only way I'd ever survive school.

Despite the negatives I endured, like the guidance counselor who said, "You won't amount too much, so don't even think about college," it was my lemonade stand moments that made all the difference. Luckily, those teachers positively influenced my life so that I did go to college – and I kept going until I earned my Ph.D. at Boston College. Mr. Tracy, my high school art teacher, is the reason I pursued an art history degree as an undergraduate. When I pursued my graduate studies and teaching license, I modeled my teaching style around Mrs. Lane, Mr. McGrath, Mrs. Cronin, Mrs. Howard and Ms. Loeb. Mr. Mac, my high school soccer coach, instilled all the things I love about being part of a team and his words and actions inform my current work around digital sportsmanship.

I'll be forever grateful to these mentors who took the time to help me embrace my innate curiosity, wonder, and awe and proudly go to the tune of my own drum. Without realizing it at the time, their willingness to stop at my lemonade stand was their way to not only personalize the learning process for me, but to help me realize what I perceived as my greatest weakness was actually my greatest strength.

What I've Learned About Lemonade Stands & Schools

What I've learned since I first started my teaching career as a middle school teacher is that making a choice to stop at a lemonade stand is really about taking a risk because you never actually know how the lemonade will actually taste before you buy it. Will it be too watery or tart or sweet? Anyone who chooses to stop understands there's no guarantee before paying for their lemonade. Why do we stop? We could be thirsty, but we could also stop because we want to support young people in their creative entrepreneurial endeavors. But, most importantly, we buy a cup of lemonade because we remember the grown ups in our own lives who consistently showed up and as a direct result, we continue to pay it forward.

Imagine if our schools were more like lemonade stands? We would create more opportunities to celebrate each and every student. More lemonade stand moments in school would encourage students to show up just as they are (whether they are too watery or tart or sweet) and just like the kids at the lemonade stand who fist pump and cheer after each sale, the same kind of enthusiasm would apply every time a grown up in school acknowledges and values their unique gifts and talents.

I could share countless stories from my years as a middle school teacher, but I'll share an example from my ten years as an associate professor in higher education as a reminder that adult learners need lemonade stand moments too. As an untraditional learner, there should be no surprise that I'm also an untraditional teacher. I taught both undergraduate and graduate students in our teacher education program and I always spent the first class building community. I never reviewed the syllabus in class. What I did instead was set up 1:1 office hours where we reviewed course expectations and personalized both the assessments and due dates. Why should everyone complete the same assignment on the same day?

My nana always used to say that cream only rises as high as the bar is set and I want to encourage you to set the bar high for your students and your colleagues too.

The Need To Take Inventory & Make Some Changes

Hopefully, classrooms no longer ask students to read every other paragraph out loud, but I know there are still classrooms that publicly display red, yellow, and green charts where students' behaviors are reported and charted throughout the day. How does this practice motivate students who are generally parked in the yellow and red zones? It doesn't. All it does is continue to separate students into us versus them categories and I can tell you from experience that students rise to the expectations that grown ups set for them. If our teachers only see us as yellow and red students, you better believe that we end up being the very best yellow and red students you've ever seen.

There are constant reminders in our schools that the one-size fits all approach towards learning excludes and fails students just like me. In fact, I saw this post on social media today and cringed because it's like we are sending the message to students do things just like everyone else – to color the exact same way, to use the same color for the sun, and no matter what, not to color outside the lines or leave any blank spaces.

The chart paper on the next pages says: **What does good coloring look like?**

Underneath that question are three examples:
1. We use colors that make sense, with three examples including a blue sun that is crossed out; a yellow, red, and black sun that is crossed out; and an orange sun.

2. We stay in the lines, with three examples of trees including one with a bubble tree top that is not colored in at all and is crossed out; a bubble tree with the trunk colored in brown and is crossed out; and a bubble tree top colored in green and a trunk colored in brown. 3. We don't leave white spaces, with three examples of hearts including one half colored orange heart; a lightly colored pink heart that is not completely colored; and a red heart completely colored in and within the lines.

What message does this send? As an untraditional learner, I can tell you that this would have told me that my way of coloring is the wrong way and that this grown up is definitely not going to stop at my lemonade stand. Imagine if the poster celebrated all the unique and creative ways to color? This is what I want to encourage you to do as you read this book. Start to take inventory back in your schools to notice opportunities to be more inclusive. If learning is not accessible for all learners, then we are excluding them from the magic that happens in classrooms.

Create More Lemonade Stand Moments

During my professional career, I have served as an associate professor, a middle school teacher, and a principal, as well as my current work at the Digital

Citizenship Institute (DCI) (https://digcitinstitute.com). In all of these roles, my struggles as a learner inform my work as we create and design learning experiences to #UseTech4Good at school, home, play, and work. Our intergenerational programs invite an entire school community to turn negatives into positives and transform school community members into designers, creative thinkers, global collaborators, change makers, problem solvers, and justice-oriented digital citizens.

Be sure to add more lemonade moments during the school day with a particular focus around how to be inclusive around how to respectfully recognize multiple viewpoints and engage with others online with respect and empathy. I also invite you to continue to explore ways to be more inclusive by following my dear friend and colleague, Jordyn Zimmerman (https://www.jordynzimmerman.com). Her work at The Nora Project (https://thenoraproject.ngo) is our go-to resource for all things regarding accessibility and inclusion at the DCI.

Graduation day at Boston College with Marialice wearing her dad's maroon doctoral robes, smiling in front of an eagle statue

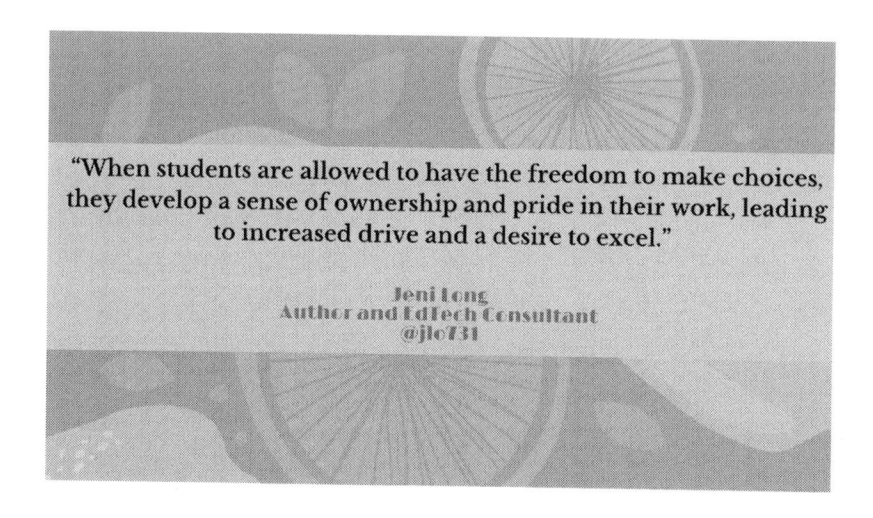

"When students are allowed to have the freedom to make choices, they develop a sense of ownership and pride in their work, leading to increased drive and a desire to excel."

Jeni Long
Author and EdTech Consultant
@jlo731

Chapter 13

The Paradigm Shift in Education Navigating the Evolution of Learning

Thank you Laurie and Marialice for sharing your voice. Besides being good friends, they are impactful educators.

Education has always been the cornerstone of societal progress, empowering individuals with knowledge, skills, and critical thinking abilities. However, the education landscape has been profoundly transformed in recent years, driven by technological advancements, changing societal needs, and a reevaluation of traditional teaching methods. This educational paradigm shift reshapes how knowledge is imparted, acquired, and applied.

Over the past few decades, technology has revolutionized nearly every aspect of human life, and education is no exception. The digital revolution has democratized information, enabling learners to access a wealth of knowledge at their fingertips. Online platforms, video lectures, interactive simulations, and educational apps have created new avenues for learning beyond the confines of traditional classrooms. Additionally, artificial intelligence (AI) and machine learning enable personalized learning experiences. Adaptive learning platforms analyze students' performance and tailor content to their needs, ensuring more efficient and effective learning outcomes.

The traditional education model often relied on passive learning, where students received information from teachers. The paradigm shift emphasizes active learning, encouraging students to engage, question, and apply their knowledge. Collaborative projects, discussions, problem-solving activities, and experiential learning are gaining prominence. Active learning enhances understanding and nurtures essential skills like critical thinking, communication, and teamwork – highly valued in the modern job market. The information age has reduced the significance of rote memorization. Instead of memorizing facts and figures, the focus is shifting toward teaching students how to think critically and solve complex problems. Education is becoming more conceptual, encouraging students to understand the underlying principles that govern various phenomena. This shift is aligned with the needs of a rapidly changing world, where adaptability and analytical thinking are crucial for success.

The job market is evolving, with automation and AI reshaping the employment landscape. As a result, there is a growing emphasis on teaching skills resilient to automation – skills that machines cannot easily replicate. These include creativity, emotional intelligence, adaptability, and cross-disciplinary thinking. Educational institutions are reevaluating their curricula to ensure graduates are equipped with the skills necessary to thrive in an unpredictable future.

While the paradigm shift in education holds immense promise, it has challenges. Access to technology, particularly in disadvantaged regions, remains a significant hurdle. Ensuring equal opportunities for quality education is a pressing concern. Moreover, the rapid pace of technological advancement requires educators to stay updated and adapt their teaching methods. The shift from traditional teaching roles to facilitators of active learning demands new skills and approaches.

As education transforms, the role of educators is shifting from being the sole source of information to becoming mentors, guides, and facilitators. Educators now focus on creating engaging learning environments, guiding students through learning, and providing personalized support. This evolution demands professional development and a shift in mindset within the teaching community. The traditional examination-centric approach is giving way to more holistic forms of assessment. Portfolios, project-based evaluations, and real-world simulations assess students' ability to apply knowledge in practical scenarios. This aligns better with the skills needed in the real world and accurately represents a student's capabilities.

Looking ahead, the paradigm shift in education could lead to the emergence of lifelong learning ecosystems. Education may become more personalized, continuous, and accessible throughout one's life. Micro-credentials, nano-degrees, and flexible learning paths could replace the traditional four-year degree model. Virtual reality and augmented reality might become integral tools, creating immersive learning experiences that transcend the limitations of physical classrooms.

The paradigm shift in education is reshaping the foundations of learning, driven by technology, changing societal needs, and reevaluating educational goals. As we navigate this transformation, it is imperative to ensure equitable access to quality education, embrace active learning, and cultivate skills that are relevant to the future. Educators, policymakers, and stakeholders must collaborate to harness the potential of this shift while addressing its challenges. By doing so, we can shape an educational landscape that empowers individuals to thrive in an ever-evolving world.

Too often in our profession we point out issues without solutions and then those issues just turn into complaints. I wanted to share what I've learned about the importance of student independence, but also give some solutions I've seen in the field.

The next sections are written by solution-providers whose products embrace student creation, entrepreneurship, and learning evolution. I asked them to share some ideas and tools to take the ideas from this book and bring them to life.

"I believe student independence is the key to unlocking the true power of learning, as it gives students a voice and choice in their education. When students have the freedom to choose and explore, they not only develop critical thinking and creativity but also take ownership of their learning journey. This makes education meaningful and unforgettable, mirroring a journey they embark on with excitement and purpose."

Greta Sandler
Learning Innovation Leader
@gret

Chapter 14

Avenues for Student Independence

We are Stronger Together

Unlocking Student Success by Respecting Failure

By Adam Bellow

Breakout EDU

An old proverb says, "Nothing ventured, nothing gained." There's certainly a lot of truth to that. It's a large part of what drives many entrepreneurs to believe that taking risks is a key and vital part of finding success. Without taking risks, we travel a safe and relatively defined path. Educators often will speak about student voice and student choice yet the system of education tends toward rewarding and applauding students for following a specific path with clearly defined outcomes, often characterized by graded work in most traditional school settings.

Empowering students to take charge of their own learning and helping them to understand that they can be creators and entrepreneurs and truly create and do anything that they can put their minds to is one of the most important lessons we can imbue children with today.

Getting comfortable with the idea that you could be wrong or that failure is not only possible but often necessary on the pathway to creating something new is not necessarily easy for students today. Risk is something we often school out of children at a very young age. Students often say, "I don't want to fail!" We have married the concept of failure with something bad instead of teaching students to embrace that trying and failing is part of learning and growing. Ironically, we want to stress the importance of "thinking outside the box" but expect the students to comply with a defined structure of what success means. That is where Breakout EDU (BreakoutEDU.com) literally and figuratively comes into play.

Stemming from the concept of an escape room game where players are forced to solve complex problems to free themselves from a locked room, Breakout EDU explores the idea but attaches academic content to each physical or digital lock that the students need to solve to complete the objective.

Thinking of failure and the promotion of trying a new idea, a lock provides concrete feedback to the learner whenever a combination is entered and tried. When students pull on a lock or enter the combination they think will advance the digital game, they are met with immediate success or failure. The screen going red and shaking gently is the same as a teacher saying "Incorrect" or the student receiving negative results on a test or assignment. Essentially, the computer or the padlock they hold tells them, "You are wrong." However, by changing the construct from a test or assignment to a game with an element of the story or a countdown timer and allowing the students to work with one another to achieve an outcome, students look beyond the momentary frustration and are determined to try again. In a Breakout EDU game, students can be wrong as often as they need to be on their path to being right. It manifests the concept of failing forward and building real grit and perseverance, even when obstacles are in the way.

Children need to be encouraged to take risks and not allow themselves to be stalled out by mistakes. These are bound to occur in school, in their career, and in life. There are choices we make that ultimately are not the right ones and we may face consequences that are not desired. Learning how to move forward and learn from experience makes one successful.

Something else important for schools to embrace is to allow teachers to see multiple sides of their learners. Students, like all people, are not exactly the same, and the things that make them unique and the strengths and weaknesses that each possess provide value when trying to solve problems and produce anything of value. Honoring each learner for who they are and what they can bring to the table, is truly important. Within a Breakout EDU game, students of all abilities are asked to work together to help the team succeed. This is a direct dichotomy to a popular game mechanic where students compete to solve multiple-choice quiz problems the fastest. Our games provide students with an experience where they are asked to work together and prove that we as a team are smarter than any individual. This is a valuable skill for entrepreneurship. While we may romanticize or celebrate the rare sole founder of a company or a handful of visionaries and moguls of business, the truth is that one of the most important skills we can develop - even in building one's strength in leadership - is that we can do more as a team. Or as Matthew Joseph has said, we are "Stronger Together."

One of the things I find most fascinating when watching students play any sort of Breakout game is that you truly get to see the learning and the interpersonal skills developing through their game playing. Some students have the right answer but are afraid to try it. Alternatively, some students are so confident that they are right that they take charge and ultimately are shown to be wrong multiple times. One observes that these two types of students and a wide range of other thinkers and behaviors begin to work together to help solve the common goal.

We can take many things from this type of experience as educators. Developing and encouraging those soft skills that students need both in and out of classrooms is greatly important. These skills allow them to process and deal with failure and success. There are many times that students are incorrect. This could be when raising their hand and answering questions in class or on a test. The key is to cultivate the right thinking around failure and give the attempt to try something the beautiful respect it deserves. Being wrong is bound to happen often on the pathway to being correct.

If we create a culture where we embrace failure and we encourage students to try and know that they can always try again or be better the next time around, we are ultimately going to create an environment, whether in the classroom or outside of it, that will surely see better results over time because we have created a populous that is not afraid to try to be one's best and yet then try again to be even better.

Creating a business, a piece of art, or anything we put into the world is an opportunity for us to grow and share. There is always a strong chance that people will not like or understand what we put out there. There is a chance that a business will fail or that the attempt to try out for the sports team or school musical will lead to disappointment. That said, creating something new can also lead to real growth for the creator and for those who experience any of their creations.

One unique way that Breakout EDU tries to empower students is to provide them the opportunity to be creators. Our platform has a tool that allows students to become game designers. They can flip the model of being a player of a Breakout game and use their content knowledge combined with their creativity to design a game that will challenge their peers. Students often love to learn that the exact same tools that we provide them to design games are available to their teachers and in fact, they are the exact same tools that the team at the company uses to build all of the games they may have played as well. There are no features that we strip away for even the youngest learners because of the deep belief that students are capable and that the best way to learn creative skills is through practice. When a student designs a game, their teacher can provide feedback and ask them for a revision, but the ability to improve things is built into the feedback loop. It's exactly the same process that we take in our company. Try something new, get feedback, and make it better.

Providing access to real-world experiences and not just playing pretend encourages students to embrace and develop their own entrepreneurial spirit. It takes a leap of faith for the students to try and know they may fail. It also takes a change in the academic culture that traditional schools embraced for many many generations. We are far more than the grades on a test, and trying and failing is far more important than being stopped by some momentary failure on an exam, an essay, or any sort of finite measurement. As Vince Lombardi famously said, "It doesn't matter how many times you get knocked down, but how many times you get back up."

Check out Breakout EDU
https://breakoutedu.com

Adam Bellow is a dedicated educational technologist and father of two young boys. Adam is the CEO and Co-Founder of Breakout EDU, the immersive gaming platform that helps teachers and students unlock the love of learning in their classrooms. Before Breakout, Adam was a Presidential Innovation Fellow for the Obama White House. Over the past decade and a half, Bellow has created several popular edtech learning platforms, including eduTecher, eduClipper, and WeLearnedIt. Bellow has written several books about educational technology, has served as a long-time board member for the EdCamp Foundation, and spoken internationally about education and the power of technology to enhance learning.

Creating Student APPreneurs

By: Alefiya Master, Founder & CEO, MAD-learn

Welcome to a journey that redefines student engagement and empowers young minds to consume and create technology. In this chapter, we will delve into the dynamic world of MAD-learn. This revolutionary platform instills an entrepreneurial mindset in students while guiding them to craft real products through mobile apps. I'm Alefiya Master, the founder and CEO of MAD-learn. I'm excited to share with you how we harness the power of mobile technology to foster innovation, creativity, and entrepreneurship among students.

MAD-learn bridges education and entrepreneurship, equipping students with the skills, mindset, and tools they need to succeed in the digital era. Our platform teaches students the language of mobile apps and empowers them to create impactful products that resonate with their peers and communities. Through our focus on the design thinking process and the philosophy of an entrepreneurial mindset, we inspire students to embrace their role as innovators and creators, ready to shape the future. Through mobile app development, we impart skills that transcend coding, including critical thinking, teamwork, empathy, and resilience. Our journey is not just about creating apps; it's about fostering a generation of thinkers, creators, and innovators who can steer the course of their future.

Design Thinking Awakens the Entrepreneurial Spirit

The six-step design thinking process is central to our approach, which guides students through creativity, planning, designing, building, testing, and launching. This process enables students to empathize with their potential users, define the problem they aim to solve, brainstorm creative solutions, prototype their app, test it with users, and finally, bring it to life. The iterative nature of this process nurtures resilience and adaptability, essential traits of successful entrepreneurs.

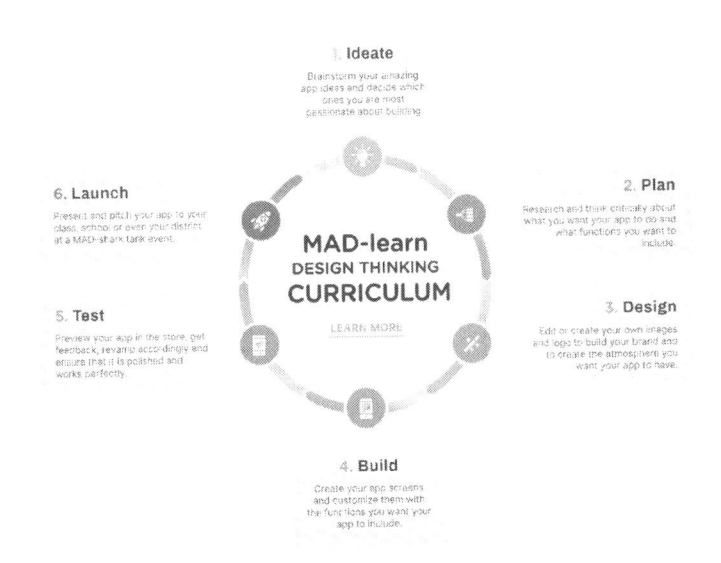

Ideate: Brainstorm your amazing app ideas and decide which ones you are most passionate about building and that the world needs the most. Create the things you wish existed!

Plan: Research and think critically about what you want your app to do and what functions you want to include. Draw out a mind map to help you organize your thoughts.

Design: Edit or create your own images and logo to build your brand and create the aesthetic and style you want your app to have.

Build: Create your app screens using lots of code, or no code at all, and program them to do what you want.

Test: Instantly preview your app on your computer or phone, get feedback, iterate, make it better, revamp it accordingly, and ensure that it is polished and works perfectly.

Launch: Present and pitch your app to your class, school, district, or even a state-wide or national app competition or a MAD-shark tank event.

As an entrepreneur, I understand the value of demystifying technology. That's why MAD-learn's approach doesn't merely focus on coding or technical jargon. Instead, we guide students through a comprehensive process encapsulating the entire app development lifecycle. By doing so, we empower students to turn their ideas into tangible solutions, bridging the gap between innovation and execution. Most importantly, the process engages ALL students— not just those who self-select into a computer science class— by teaching them to create technology instead of just consuming it.

MAD-learn isn't just about creating traditional entrepreneurs; it's about fostering a mindset of innovation and resourcefulness in all students, regardless of their aspirations. We believe in the power of every student to #beapreneur, anypreneur who seizes opportunities, challenges the status quo, drives change in various capacities, innovates, and takes charge of their future. Whether they start their own business or innovate within an existing one, the entrepreneurial mindset we cultivate through MAD-learn equips students to succeed in an ever-changing world.

Mobile is the Ultimate Hook

We live in a tech-driven world where being a passive consumer of technology is simply not enough. The ability to comprehend how technology functions and to construct it provides an edge that sets students apart. With MAD-learn, we aim to instill the essential skills needed for success in this landscape, equipping students with the tools to create, innovate, and solve real-world challenges.

The power to conceptualize, construct, and comprehend technology gives students a distinct edge in today's competitive landscape. However, this is more than just a practical advantage; it's a way of thinking that cultivates resilience, resourcefulness, and innovation. MAD-learn's mission is to nurture creators of technology – individuals who not only grasp how technology operates and contribute to its evolution.

In an age where mobile devices have become an integral part of our daily lives, they serve as the ultimate hook to capture the attention of young minds. These devices are not merely tools for communication; they are gateways to a world of endless possibilities. Consider this: when did you last meet a student unfamiliar with a smartphone and mobile apps? These applications have transcended being novelties to becoming the language through which students interact with the world. From social networking to gaming and entertainment education, mobile apps have seamlessly integrated into every facet of modern existence. In 2020, there were just over 14 billion mobile devices worldwide. We now have 17 billion devices on the planet, projected to rise to 18 billion by just 2025. MAD-learn harnesses students' familiarity with apps and transforms it into a powerful educational tool.

We recognize the allure of mobile technology and utilize it as a catalyst to awaken the entrepreneurial spirit within students. In today's rapidly evolving digital landscape, our phones capture our attention, seamlessly integrate into every aspect of our lives, connect us to the world like never before, and offer unparalleled opportunities for innovation. I am thrilled to guide you through our innovative approach to nurturing the entrepreneurial mindset within students and helping them create real products in the form of mobile apps. We have captured the power of mobile technology to provide students with a platform to understand and use apps and become creators of these transformative tools.

Our platform enables students to be adept users of apps and creators of these digital solutions. By speaking the language of apps fluently, students can now channel their ideas, creativity, and problem-solving skills into building their own mobile applications. The process of creativity, planning, designing, building, testing, and launching their products becomes an authentic and immersive learning experience that prepares them for the demands of an ever-evolving tech landscape. This transformation enhances students' technical skills and cultivates a mindset of innovation and problem-solving, key attributes of successful entrepreneurs.

A study conducted by the New Zealand Ministry of Education concluded the following:

When students make apps, they learn:
- valuable STEAM skills like coding, programming, graphic design, and content creation"
- how to solve real-world problems with digital design.

Whether tackling challenges at school, within the community, or even on a global scale – knowing how to build apps empowers students to change their environment through technological intervention meaningfully."

Using app development as a context for learning in your classroom, you can explore the technological areas – in particular:
- digital technologies
- computational thinking for digital technologies

- designing and developing digital outcomes
- design and visual communication

Think about how developing an app can be integrated across different curriculum learning areas and support students' digital literacy."

More research in support of mobile app development in the classroom can be found here:

Students Do The Talking

The true essence of MAD-learn lies in the stories of students who transformed their aspirations into reality. Let's explore a few inspiring examples of student-made mobile apps that showcase the depth of creativity and impact that our platform encourages:

Uncut: This app was created by high school students in Camilla, GA. UnCut is an app to give those who self-harm an outlet to find healthy alternatives to self-harming, support hotlines, inspirational stories. and reasons not to self-harm. A powerful app that addresses a tough issue. It demonstrates our students' depth of understanding of the importance of mental health support and bringing difficult issues to the forefront instead of pushing them under a rug.

Pollution: A middle school student in Palm Beach County, FL recognized the lack of accessible information about the environmental impact of pollution on different animals. Motivated by this issue, this student created an app that even includes a section on sea turtle tracking so users can track their migratory patterns to learn more about sea turtles and the threats they face —and thus become compelled to protect them. In this student's own words, "This app can help you learn more about pollution. And more than you could ever learn in school. In school they just teach you how pollution is bad and how you can help. But in this app you can learn about greenhouse gasses, carbon footprints, sharks and turtles affected by pollution, and more. In my 11 years of living I've never seen an app like mine, where you can learn about pollution and I felt I needed to change that so I made this app for genuinely curious people."

Birdmaker: This app was created as an fun and enjoyable artistic outlet to create different styles of birds by a middle school student in Cobb County, GA. You can create birds wearing hats, birds that are happy, birds in frog costumes. This student describes their app: "The point of this app is primarily for fun and just personal enjoyment. The app is mainly if you want to make a little decoration or cute thing then you can do that. A variety of nice options are made for you to enjoy. I hope that you like it! You may use anything you make, just please credit the app. There should be 180 total combinations. Thanks for using my app!"

Refugees: Recognizing the challenges faced by refugees in Atlanta, Georgia, a middle student designed an app to improve our understanding of the history and reality of the Bolivarian Diaspora. "This app is meant to educate people about this refugee crisis, with the hope of helping the future Venezuelans. The pictures, videos, articles, and activities are meant to hopefully impact you, and let you take away this information to share it with others." By addressing a genuine need, students not only enhanced the lives of refugees in the city, but also provided much-needed context and information for host residents. You can see this student's "Planning Phase" here:

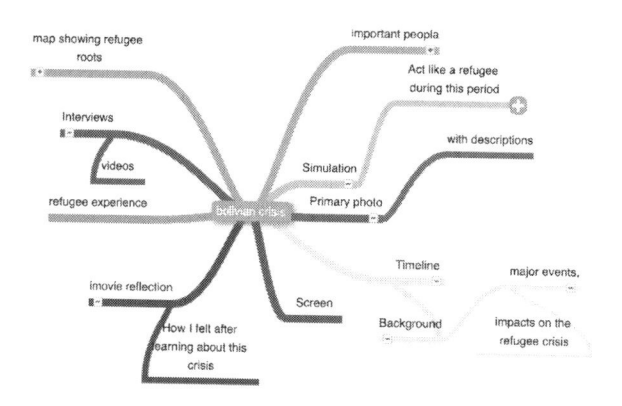

Providing Real-world Experience

MAD-learn also has a Virtual Internship Program for middle and high school students. Since we have a global team with team members in three countries and five states, we invite students to become an immersed part of our team to learn new skills, sharpen existing ones, and do real work that matters to the company - all from the comfort of their own home or classroom. This transformative educational experience bridges the gap between classroom learning and practical skills. Designed to empower students with hands-on knowledge, this program offers a unique opportunity to engage with real-world projects and industry professionals from the comfort of their own space. The program's flexibility also allows students from various backgrounds to participate and thrive.

Through a diverse range of disciplines, MAD-learn's virtual internships provide immersive learning experiences that cultivate creativity, problem-solving, and collaboration. With a commitment to personalized mentorship, participants receive guidance from experts in their chosen fields, enhancing their professional growth.

Applications for MAD-learn's Virtual Internship program are open on a rolling basis but are limited to students who have first experienced MAD-learn in a classroom setting. You can learn more about the internship by scanning this QR code.

Real-world success stories of MAD-learn interns exemplify the program's impact. "Interning with MAD-learn has been a great and rewarding experience because I get to work directly with the CEO and build a relationship with everyone around me," Aarush L., a former intern, shared. "My experience so far at MAD-learn has been great because everything that I needed to do was clear and everyone has been very helpful & welcoming," says Syeda T. a current intern. Another intern, Darius W., mentioned, "So far it's been great, I've learned so much about the MAD-learn community and its values. I love that I learn about different cultures while being in the comfort of my own home."

With each student who successfully navigates the MAD-learn experience, a new chapter in the story of empowerment is written. I am filled with pride as I witness the transformative journeys of students who were once learners and are now creators. Each mobile app they create is a testament to their ingenuity, resilience, and commitment to shaping the future. Together, we are nurturing a generation of creators, innovators, and problem solvers who are not just prepared for the challenges of the future but are actively driving its transformation.
#Beapreneur, Anypreneur

It's not often that you find a millennial, minority, female educator-turned-entrepreneur who has founded and grown two EdTech companies that now impact over 50,000 students in 30 states and five countries, successfully raised investment for her businesses, grown a global team, and fights for what students need in schools today.

I believe that communities with greater collaboration between all stakeholders result in higher academic and social outcomes, stronger values, and increased future success for students. My degree in psychology and education from Emory University, along with my training and experience as a Montessori educator, power my passion for wide-scale education improvement. This passion led me to start my first education company in 2011 to enable schools to better communicate with and engage their communities through mobile. I am now focusing on bringing the concepts and tools of app development to K-12 students by enabling them to build mobile apps through the 6-step design thinking process with my second EdTech company, MAD-learn.

I want to encourage you and your students to "#beapreneur, anypreneur" through the entrepreneurial lessons we have learned. Pick what gives you energy, excites you, and makes your heart beat just a little faster, and then figure out how to innovate, disrupt, do better, bolder things. All jobs are at high risk of automation and disruption through AI in the next few decades. When we don't know what jobs will exist 10 years from now, we have to teach kids to create their own!

The philosophy of #beapreneur transcends the traditional boundaries of entrepreneurship. It's about empowering students to recognize their potential, take calculated risks, and contribute positively to society. Whether they envision themselves as founders of startups or catalysts of change within established organizations, the entrepreneurial mindset nurtured by MAD-learn equips them to thrive in an era defined by constant disruption.

As we continue to witness the extraordinary achievements of students using MAD-learn, I am filled with immense pride and excitement for the entrepreneurial journey ahead for each of them. Together, we are building a generation of empowered individuals who are prepared to make their mark on the world, one mobile app at a time. So, here's to the students who dare to imagine, to innovate, and to #beapreneur – for they are the architects of a future that knows no bounds, a future where technology is harnessed to create, to impact, and to thrive. In the tapestry of modern education and entrepreneurship, MAD-learn weaves a thread that empowers students to seize the possibilities of tomorrow. We want to help you bridge the gap between learning and doing, equipping students with the skills, mindset, and resources they need to thrive in a dynamic and ever-evolving digital landscape.

iBlocks
Project-Based Learning

A Project Based Learning Solution: iBlocks

By Robert Abraham

Education is evolving to meet the dynamic needs of modern society, and as a result, traditional teaching methods are being replaced by more student-centered and interactive strategies. One such pedagogical approach gaining momentum in the classroom is project-based learning (PBL). PBL shifts the focus from passive learning to active engagement by posing a question or problem that students must work to solve. This allows students to take control of their education and become active problem-solvers. A great example of PBL in action is iBlocks. iBlocks, or 'instructional Blocks,' engage students in authentic learning experiences in which they apply their knowledge to solve real-world problems. They allow students to work on complex issues while developing critical thinking, problem-solving, and collaboration skills. iBlocks encourage students to become creators and independent learners and empower them to take ownership of their education. As an Instructional Strategist, I assist teachers and facilitate the process.

I have seen firsthand many examples of students engaged while working on iBlocks. Many schools purchased 3D printers but struggled to integrate them into their curriculum. One of my favorite iBlocks, Tiny Houses, meets this need effectively. Students work together to learn about energy efficiency and how tiny houses can address efficiency concerns. The culminating project has students design and build a tiny house with their 3D printer. In one school I worked with, some of the students could not effectively work with the software needed to build models for the 3D printer. The flexibility of the iBlock allowed those students to use construction paper, tape and cardboard to build their tiny house and be included in the project. Teachers need to be flexible with their large class sizes and the varied learning levels of the students, and iBlocks, like any good PBL activity, offer them this flexibility. iBlocks also let them work on the soft skills students desperately need to succeed.

Project-based learning gives students autonomy over their learning journey. During PBL, students have the freedom to demonstrate their understanding and approach content in a way that appeals to their interests and passions. This autonomy fosters intrinsic motivation, as students are more invested in projects they personally care about. As they make decisions on project topics, goals, and methods, they become active participants in their education, which can significantly enhance their learning experience. Furthermore, the

Avenues for Student Independence

autonomy provided by PBL encourages students to take responsibility for their work and outcomes. They must manage their time effectively, set deadlines, and develop organizational skills to complete their projects successfully. This sense of ownership nurtures a growth mindset, where students see challenges as opportunities for growth and view failures as stepping stones to success as they understand it is okay to "fail forward."

As with any PBL method, iBlocks are student-led and teacher-guided. Students follow the engineering design process of researching, constructing, testing, evaluating, and redesigning as they work toward a capstone project. The first step is to meet with the school to determine the needs of the students and focus on the skills that need improvement. Each iBlock includes everything needed to implement it effectively in the classroom. This includes a framework that aligns to local, state, and national standards. There are also supportive materials, like the teacher's guide and lesson plans, to help teachers implement an iBlock successfully. To facilitate autonomy, iBlocks also come with questions and prompts to guide students, allowing them to keep a journal of their work while self-reflecting. There are dozens of iBlocks titles to choose from with topics ranging from robotics and computer science to building literacy and inventive storytelling.

A great example of the impact of iBlocks as a PBL tool can be seen in my work with a group of fourth- and fifth-grade students in Brooklyn, New York. These students previously struggled with focusing on their schoolwork and completing their assignments. They were being supported in a traditional classroom setting, and their teacher and I worked together to redesign an after-school experience to improve their soft skills by engaging them in a cooperative learning experience.

With the abundance of STEM technologies available to the school, we decided to structure our PBL activity around the KIBO robot. From our catalog of iBlocks PBL activities, the teacher selected the Class Pet project. In this project, students learned about different class pets, then chose a robot to represent a particular pet. The teacher and the students chose the KIBO robot for this project. My role was to facilitate and assist the teacher and the students in coding the KIBO class pet for the culminating activity, a class pet robot parade.

The student worked with the teacher on the first phases of the iBlock which consisted of research and exploration of different class pets followed by a presentation of their findings. The students then worked on persuasive arguments as to why their pet should be chosen and pitched the ideas to the teacher. At this point, it was time for them to design the costumes for the KIBO pets and begin the coding portion of the project. The students were engaged in every step of the iBlock activity and looked forward to coding their pets and the upcoming robot parade.

At the program's start, we experienced some challenges as the students had difficulties staying on task and working together as a group. We defined clear roles within each group for the students and the modules of the iBlocks allowed us to present the tasks to the students as mini-assignments with easily reachable goals. To inspire creativity, the students were given various research options from traditional encyclopedias to online resources. They were also given voice and choice by choosing how to present their findings. Some chose Google Slides, others Microsoft Sway, etc.

Some clear "wins" also let us know our project was moving in the right direction for the students. The students became more engaged as they completed each module and their associated tasks. The students who were a little more advanced with their coding skills assisted the others in the group. The school's assistant principal told me that she observed a change in the students' attitudes and behavior and wanted to discuss other iBlocks for the coming school year.

At the end of the program, the students culminated their Class Pet project with a robot parade. They dressed their robot up to look like their chosen pet and choreographed a parade route in the gym. The teachers and administrators that were present were amazed with the students' engagement and excitement and it was a wonderful experience. Here are some photos of the project:

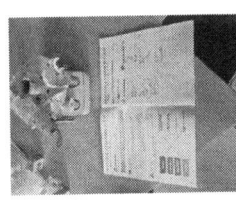

In traditional classrooms, success is often measured by grades on exams. Students may be taught to fear failure and avoid challenges. iBlocks and other PBL activities, focusing on continuous improvement, instill the belief that setbacks are part of the learning process and should be embraced as opportunities to learn and grow. Furthermore, students often memorize information for exams but don't always grasp its practical applications. PBL, on the other hand, demands a deeper understanding of the subject matter since students need to apply their knowledge to authentic situations. This enhances their critical thinking skills and enables them to see the relevance of their learning. iBlocks are designed around real-world scenarios so that they encounter complex challenges that require thoughtful analysis and innovative solutions. This will benefit students in academic and professional settings.

The skills needed in professional settings need to be fostered throughout a student's education. Creativity and innovation are important skills in the classroom and in the job market. iBlocks encourages students to think creatively while also allowing them to explore multiple perspectives and propose innovative solutions. The flexibility of iBlocks and other PBL activities gives students more ownership of their work. Project-based learning often involves interdisciplinary learning, which develops a comprehensive understanding of concepts and prepares students for the complexity of real-world challenges. With many topics, iBlocks offers teachers many options to engage their students across all grade levels and subject areas.

Another benefit of project-based learning is its emphasis on collaboration. In PBL, students often work in teams versus the traditional classroom of individual student worksheets. This collaboration is more representative of real-life work scenarios. An iBlock encourages the exchange of ideas, the division of tasks, and the implementation of diverse perspectives to tackle complex problems. While working on an iBlock, students learn essential social and emotional skills such as effective communication, empathy, and conflict resolution. In the after-school Class Pet iBlock I mentioned above, the students were from different classes and even grades, yet they could work well together in groups based on their choice of pets. By allowing them to group by choice rather than by assignment, they worked happily together in a cooperative manner. Collaborative projects also foster a sense of community within the classroom. Students develop a supportive and inclusive learning environment as they work together towards a common goal. In this environment, differences are respected, and everyone's contributions are valued, leading to a positive classroom culture that encourages active engagement and participation.

Project-based learning is a powerful educational approach that empowers students by providing them with autonomy while fostering collaboration, enhancing critical thinking, promoting creativity, and building confidence. In a world where adaptability and problem-solving skills are essential, PBL gives students the tools they need to excel academically and professionally. The Class Pet iBlock allowed a group of students from Brooklyn to collaborate and create wonderful projects culminating in a successful robot parade. By implementing iBlocks in classrooms, educators can create a stimulating and inclusive learning environment which I was fortunate to witness first hand. PBL with iBlocks will empower students to take charge of their education and become lifelong learners. For more information, please visit iblocks.teq.com or www.teq.com

Empowering Student Discovery with Marty the Robot

By the Robotical Team

There's one sure-fire way to grab students' attention in the classroom: unboxing Marty the Robot. I have witnessed it firsthand and heard countless similar reports from other educators: there's always a swell of excitement and enthusiasm when students see Marty for the first time. While their reaction is entirely spontaneous, Robotical has very deliberately set out to design a physical STEM tool that harnesses children's innate curiosity, tapping into their sense of adventure and imagination. What Robotical has done so successfully with Marty – as all the awards they have won testify – is create a product that, from the outside, looks like a very cute, approachable little robot but has the functionality to handle every stage in the K-12 CS curriculum and well beyond. Marty has the scope to extend its capabilities through integration with accessories and its range of use with cross-curricular lesson plans and activities. What this means is that learners not only embark on a progressive learning journey with Marty, it's also an individualized one. And that is vitally important when it comes to engagement and confidence building.

Suppose we start at the beginning of this journey. We know that young children live in a world where sensory experiences strongly influence their development, especially in response to visual and physical stimuli. We also know they can be quite traditional in their views of a robot's appearance. Young learners love using Marty because Marty is a mini robot version of themselves. Marty stands on two legs, and has arms and a very expressive face. Having a human form, from a design and engineering perspective, means that Marty is capable of performing so many more different types of actions than, let's say, a rolling robot, and that, in turn, makes Marty a much more appealing proposition for learners to explore. Being made out of robust plastic-molded parts means that Marty can withstand the rigors of this hands-on exploration. By possessing limbs that move independently, Marty can mimic human movements very effectively. Marty can walk, sidestep, kick, balance, wiggle, wave, and turn. What many robots fail to achieve, but Marty does rather ingeniously with a simple shift in eyebrow position, is to convey human-like emotion. So, not only do children find a likeness to themselves in Marty's appearance, they also find it in Marty's expressiveness and are consequently much quicker to form a connection.

Beyond the nuts and bolts, Marty is equipped with a surprising amount of tech, including motor position sensors, acceleration and tilt sensors, color and infrared

Avenues for Student Independence

sensors, and an extensive sound library that includes pre-recorded sounds and musical instruments as well as the ability to record custom sounds. Marty can be used alongside both micro:bit and Raspberry Pi, and improvements are released regularly on the app and then updated automatically on the users' devices. There are also periodic updates to the robots, which can be carried out over the cable (OTC) or via Bluetooth. The users handle those, with or without technical support from the Robotical team.

But it's the fun touches that make the difference for students. Each robot comes with stickers and LED disco eyes as standard. I cannot overemphasize how much the simple fact of being able to customize a Marty matters when conferring a sense of ownership for the learner. Play is an essential part of a child's cognitive development. For pre-readers, Marty operates using color cards - each color corresponding to a certain movement or motion. Learning direction is exciting when Marty navigates a dangerous maze on a colored path!

For children aged 7 to 11, who are at the point of becoming more logical about concrete and specific things, having stimulating visual and physical aids in the classroom really supports the processing of information and increases their enjoyment of what is being taught, empowering them to explore further. When introducing foundation concepts in programming, such as sequencing and the relationship between instructions and operations, the real value in Marty is that it helps learners see tangible results from abstract concepts –

Marty's reactions correspond directly and instantly to the code sequences built by the programmer. It's a simple yet very significant reward that engages the learner in a much more profound way, as one teacher described:

"Marty the Robot has been a wonderful addition to the school and has increased engagement with coding, allowing a physical and visible response to coding inputs on a device. This has helped children link with what they are doing and how successes and mistakes in coding are instantly visible. Marty encourages the development of problem-solving skills with children willing to make mistakes and then attempt to solve any problems."

Bridging the gap between unplugged coding to introductory block-based programming language, MartyBlocks Jr (based on ScratchJr) is an RC sequencer that introduces step-by-step programming without the need to drag-and-drop. It works similarly to a remote-control car or a character in a video game. It's a mechanism that many children are already familiar with, making the transition between the two stages easier to grasp for learners and more fun at the same time.

For older students getting to grips with abstract concepts, interactive tools help develop logical thought and deductive reasoning abilities through trial-and-error learning, cause-and-effect relationships, and systematic thinking. Marty offers a full progression from block-based to real-world, text-based coding languages, where the concepts (such as conditionals, loops, and variables) are carried through. Since the concepts are already familiar, the transition is less daunting.

Regarding STEM solutions, no other robot offers the breadth of learning progression, from screen-free coding and block-based programming to Python.

Teachers can watch students advance at their own pace while assessing and evaluating their progress as they learn, thanks to learning paths set out for all skill levels in a comprehensive online Learning Portal. All resources are mapped to national and regional curricula, including CSTA Education Standards (Kindergarten to G9), to enable educators to plan and deliver activities that meet success criteria, focusing on facilitating learning experiences and reporting on progress. Students can develop their creative thinking and problem-solving skills, while learning important concepts across the CS curriculum, from computational thinking to numeracy, literacy, and more. The portal contains guides and activities to incorporate Marty into other curriculum areas such as well.

One teacher told me: "I love how adaptable Marty can be and how many different topics and cross-curricular links I can make when using Marty in my lessons. It helps to bring coding off the screen and let students see their code run in real life, which makes learning to code a lot less intimidating."

Another added: "The versatility of Marty is by far the biggest draw for me. It's incredibly important that the children develop their skills in digital literacy; however, having such an engaging addition to the classroom can make a difference in so many areas – even behavior management. Many children who have additional support needs struggle with abstract learning and prefer something concrete and structured. In areas such as creative writing or any task requiring them to create something from nothing, it can be incredibly difficult for some children to get ideas from their heads and on paper. Marty allowed them to share their ideas differently and made the curriculum more accessible. The children often didn't even realize that learning was taking place because they were having so much fun."

Indeed, a growing body of evidence supports using humanoid robots in education for children with additional support needs. Robots create a non-judgemental and non-threatening environment in which students can more easily interact, as one teacher explained: "Marty has proven very beneficial when working with children with additional support needs. Our elementary school has many children with communication difficulties who struggle to express their feelings and emotions. Marty has provided an opportunity to develop communication skills with these children, who are keen to share and communicate their thoughts and feelings with him. One boy was very upset and couldn't explain why to an adult. When I introduced him to Marty he was more than willing to explain everything. Being able to code Marty to respond sympathetically to the boy surreptitiously also encouraged this interaction. Many of the children with additional support need to treat Marty as a friend and part of the class. We are only beginning to explore various possibilities to use Marty as a communications support for children."

Another key outcome is fostering strong communication skills and teamwork through collaborative learning experiences. Students who are interested and motivated in a subject are more likely to communicate with peers and teachers actively. Furthermore, as illustrated in the quote above, robots are non-judgemental and unbiased in their interactions, which makes some children who suffer from social anxiety feel more at ease. Robotical suggests a 3:1 student-to-robot ratio in the classroom, encouraging cooperative learning where students work together in small groups to achieve learning goals. This provides opportunities for students to communicate, exchange ideas, troubleshoot and split tasks, improving essential communication and teamwork skills. In working collaboratively, students can teach and help one another out – it has also been known for students to assist teachers in trying to overcome an issue or explain how to do something – which significantly affects self-confidence and self-esteem.

What Marty the Robot delivers as one of the most adaptable educational robots on the market is multifold: the gamification of learning creates an engaging and immersive environment that enhances student enjoyment, the ability to apply abstract concepts in a practical setting improves understanding and retention of knowledge, collaborative learning and group practice fosters teamwork and essential communication skills, and the analyzing and evaluating of information cultivates essential skill sets to prepare students for the future in a digital world. Marty is an all-round star turn.

Gamestormers Student Game Design

By Jon Spike

"Can we play again?"

Those four words are absolute gold to a game designer. Those four words can make years of failure, restarts, and dead ends disappear. Hearing that your creation brought enough joy to a group to warrant another round is worth every hardship that goes into a passion project. And yet, those four words do not happen on the first prototype. If you're lucky, you won't hear those words until prototype 63. However, that struggle does not deter the young creators in our classrooms.

My name is Jon Spike, and I am an educator, a game designer, and, most importantly, a father. I've had the great fortune of working with students nationwide to help them create board and card games.

One of the most impressive aspects of working with young creators is their incredible determination and willingness to press on with a design challenge. I have taught students of all ages in game design, and no matter their experience level, background, or interests, they all gravitate towards a well-planned maker activity.

For starters, students always amaze me with their game design ideas. One student in Mr. D's class created a deck of cards in the style of Magic: The Gathering for Shakespeare's Henry IV play. Every character, major event, and decision from the play came through via the cards the student created, with each ability and power reflective of concepts from Shakespeare's classic. The sheer size of the student's card deck - over sixty cards - was an incredible feat of both attention to detail and commitment to making an enjoyable game.

Another Mr. M's class student loved the group card game Two Rooms and a Boom. During a unit on the Roman Empire, the students asked if they could make a version of Two Rooms and a Boom about the assassination of Julius Caesar. After several planning spreadsheets and slide decks later, the student had a faithful adaptation of the historical event and major players, all distilled into a playable version of the game for the whole class to try.

What is the commonality between the two student stories above? Both of those learners had to have an incredible amount of knowledge about their subject matter to faithfully capture the essence of their chosen topics. In addition, both students engaged in metaphorical expression, translating the people and events of their chosen themes into playable game rules and mechanics. Both qualities showcase how much the students engaged with the materials and pushed themselves further to make an experience that their peers and teachers would enjoy.

Although individual student stories of game creation showcase the value of playful learning, the experience only multiplies when an entire class of learners begins to design games and experiences. As a game designer and educator, I have had the great honor of speaking with students before and during their game design processes to help them approach and refine their prototypes.

Although they were in New York State and I was in Wisconsin, Mr. S invited me into his classroom to talk about game design strategies with his students, along with answering questions about everything from how to design games in teams to creating games that respectfully captured the topic of the unit: World War I. I shared with the students that it is essential to represent events concerning those oppressed, victimized, and marginalized during this period. What stood out to me in the students' creations were their adherence to this concept - games focused less on the "big picture" of winning a war and more on the individual struggles the soldiers faced each day. The students chose not to glamorize war but rather portray its destructive reality, and the games relayed those themes through their gameplay.

Beyond game design, students have an incredible knack for valuable and insightful feedback regarding games and experiences. In the early development of our first game release, Gamestormers, I sent out copies to Mrs. B's middle school class in Missouri. Each playtest group was given the game rules, materials, and a form to complete with their evaluations regarding the gameplay, clarity, pacing, and overall enjoyment of the game. When I got the chance to read their written feedback and then meet with the class via video call to hear their ideas, favorite parts of the game, and recommendations for improvement, I was floored by their observations. Students noted what areas of the game caused unnecessary complications, like a currency system that did not fit. Others noted that certain actions players could take were not as interesting or powerful, which could deter players from using those choices. Most of all, the students helped me identify what worked in the game - the storytelling and creation elements. Without their spot-on feedback, Gamestormers would not be the game it is today.

No matter the age, students are storytellers and world builders at heart. During a summer enrichment course, I spoke to a group of 7, 8, and 9-year-old students about designing games and starting a business, and then taught them how to play Gamestormers. Within five minutes, those elementary students assembled five-card game narratives and designs, detailing to each other what made their games unique, how they would work, and how all their chosen elements came together in the finished product. During the hour I spent playing Gamestormers with the students, I never saw an individual who could not make a great game concept out of their selected cards - a true testament to the students' innovative thinking and creativity.

Games are not just incredibly important to the students I work with each day, but also my family. As I first developed Gamestormers, I made my soon-to-be-born daughter, Sloane, the main character and put her on the cover. Becoming a father inspired me to encourage Sloane to chase her dreams, and dedicating Gamestormers to her seemed like a fitting choice. Beyond Sloane, my niece and nephew have loved playing Gamestormers from day one, making entertaining games about dinosaurs recovering lost ice cream, princesses traveling through time to stop zombies, and much more.

I went back and forth about what to get my nephew for his birthday. He loves a good stuffed animal for his bed. His video game library could use another fun title. Perhaps an ironic t-shirt?

But my mind traveled back to the night we took a family vacation, and I showed my nephew a prototype game I was working on developing. The game was a dungeon-crawler but used toy-based versions of catapults, bows, and balls to knock over enemies in the cardboard-built cavern levels. As we played, he made suggestions and recommendations to scale up the difficulty of each level or power-ups the characters should have to make the players feel more like their game hero counterparts.

As I thought about this memory, I settled on the perfect gift: a board game design kit full of blank cards, dice, game boards, and more for him to make his own game. Within minutes of opening the gift, my nephew started thinking about the game he could make, how it would work, and why folks would want to play it endlessly.

In education and in life, the best gift we can give our youth is a blank canvas. A blank canvas is an invitation to make something incredible. I recommend challenging kids to make an experience, a moment.

Challenge them to make a game that makes others who play it say, "Can we play again?"

Learn more at: www.gamestormedu.com/gamestormers

Curiosity in the Classroom with PebbleGo Inquiry-based Learning Resources and Content Creation Tools

Capstone and PebbleGo support the implementation of inquiry-based learning in elementary school classrooms through its easily accessible platform offering nonfiction articles and various ways to extend learning through videos, activities, and timelines to kindergarten through upper elementary school students.

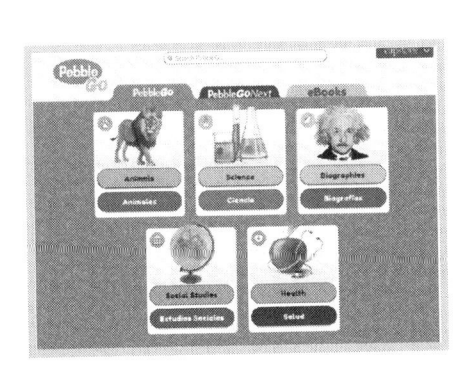

PebbleGo is a supplemental resource that integrates easily into all core curriculum approaches. Not only does it give students entry to a wide array of texts and topics, it also encourages students to explore and make meaningful decisions about their topic through an easy and intuitive platform that even the youngest students can independently navigate.

As teachers begin to encourage research strategies, PebbleGo creates an insulated and safe space for exploration and decision-making. Students can easily explore and learn new information, and teachers can also direct students to specific topics or articles to encourage young readers or engage in whole-group reading opportunities. This platform also allows students to share what they learned in PebbleGo Create through digital posters, which can be shared with teachers and classmates.

The social learning built into PebbleGo Create highlights the student's choice and voice in the research process and fosters creativity in how students share what they learned while they read. PebbleGo's vast library of facts and easily navigable articles break down large topics into learnable sections. Teachers can utilize graphic organizers and collaborative projects targeting a particular topic unit from their core text. These five flexible options invite teachers to think creatively about integrating PebbleGo into their current curriculum and build the depth of student knowledge and interest as they are introduced to different texts. PebbleGo also fits well into project-based learning and makes this type of project accessible to very young students. As students learn to navigate and search within PebbleGo's suite of tools, they are equipped to actively practice literacy skills in a digital environment through evaluation, synthesis and analysis in a single setting that is fun, exciting, and inviting.

Teachers can leverage the ease of access afforded by PebbleGo to allow students to be curious and to explore wide-ranging topics, which positions learning and exploration directly in the hands of elementary school students and fosters an inquiry stance. Research shows that when teachers prioritize student inquiry and provide appropriate support, student learning, knowledge development, and critical thinking skills increase. Thus, when teachers apply these paradigms to their implementation of PebbleGo as a supplemental instructional tool, it launches student-centered inquiry into a hands-on exploration leveraging unique features like authentic read-aloud audio, easy navigation, and age-appropriate, current content.

Teachers can encourage students to ask questions and wonder as a part of their daily routine. The teacher can select one PebbleGo article as a quick read-aloud and then direct students to write one or two questions (or more) that they now have after hearing the article. This can foster wondering and question-asking regularly and make students comfortable asking questions. Teachers can encourage students to record these questions in a daily writing journal.

Students can easily browse through the network of articles, which provide both visual and audio cues to support its use with students who are emergent or beginning readers. Additionally, PebbleGo provides a creative and flexible space for advanced learners to extend their learning through additional exploration and opportunities for upper elementary school students to peruse various exciting and relevant nonfiction articles within a safe, reliable online environment that invites curiosity and independent investigation.

Demonstrating Knowledge and Curiosity with Student-created Content

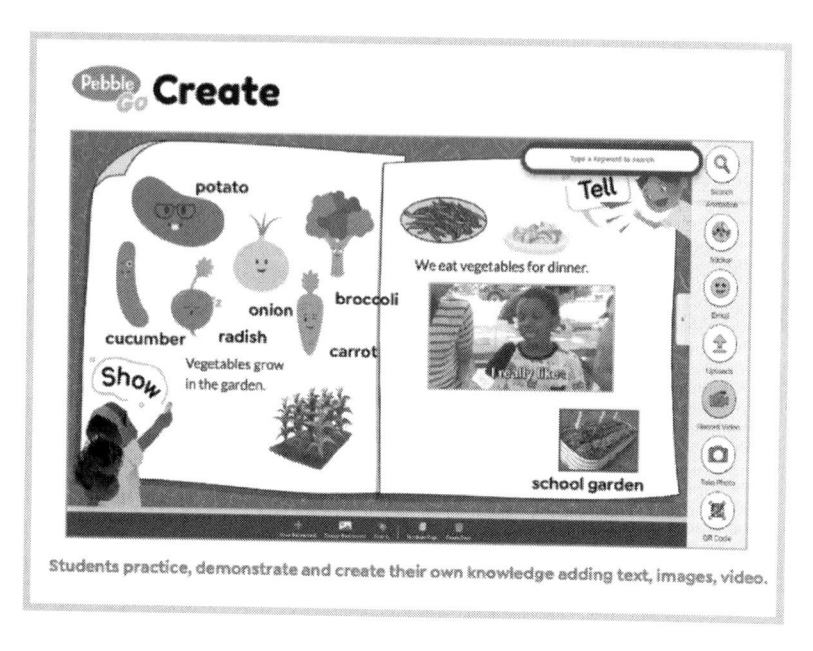

Students practice, demonstrate and create their own knowledge adding text, images, video.

PebbleGo offers not only an extensive repository of curated content and articles, it also boasts a useful creation tool, PebbleGo Create, which can enhance classroom inquiry projects as a flexible and intuitive way for students to share what they have learned in digital posters and visual representations that are appropriate and applicable at all grade levels. When paired with an inquiry-based classroom approach that emphasizes student curiosity and independent research opportunities, this tool offers a powerful solution for teachers who seek to engage students as investigators, wanderers, and self-motivated learners.

PebbleGo Create is an intuitive digital workspace for students to demonstrate learning and share their knowledge with authentic tasks. By pairing student-centered active learning with engaging curriculum-connected content, students can retain more essential concepts core to academic success.

Teachers can pair PebbleGo content or articles with the 'create' tool to allow students to share their expanded stories, thoughts, and experiences. Students can use the canvas and tools to add their own text, images, video recordings, and graphics supporting their knowledge transfer.

An example may include a daily listen-and-read exercise where students select an article. Students use headphones to listen to their article as a read-aloud on PebbleGo. Once they have listened to their selected article, students can use the audio recording feature on PebbleGo Create to explain why they selected the article and share two facts they learned and one question about the topic. As an added development of language acquisition and transition, students can hear the article in English or Spanish and practice recording what they learned in the primary or secondary language.

Students with limited English or language acquisition development can also use the PebbleGo Create tool to add imagery and language in their primary language while expanding and practicing their transition to English practice with text, audio, or video recording.

PebbleGo Create can assemble portfolios that allow students to share their learning over time. Using PebbleGo Create, teachers can gather student work in a portfolio to show their growth over time and highlight various types of assignments that ask students to engage with the text in various ways. Through a portfolio, students can self-assess their own growth, determine their strengths and interests, and understand their reading range throughout the school year.

Capstone's mission is to help students succeed by making learning fun by empowering educators and learners with rich inquiry-based learning experiences. Further, the goal is to present content in a way that expands their curiosity into a deeper learning experience whereby students not only consume content from PebbleGo but are creators of their own content and knowledge, thus encouraging a love of lifelong learning.

To learn more about Capstone resources and PebbleGo or PebbleGo Create, visit www.PebbleGo.com / www.CapstonePub.com.

Closing Thoughts

Building a Student Centered Classroom

Empowering Learners for Success

We will close this book where we started, focusing on students at the center. Whether it be a lemonade stand or in the classroom, how are you empowering learners?

The traditional classroom, characterized by a teacher-centered approach, has long been the standard in education. However, as our understanding of effective pedagogy evolves, there is a growing realization that a student-centered approach is more relevant and effective in fostering meaningful learning experiences. A student-centered classroom places learners at the heart of the educational process, recognizing their agency, interests, and diverse learning styles.

A student-centered classroom shifts the focus from the teacher as the primary disseminator of knowledge to the student as an active participant in their learning journey. The role of the teacher evolves to that of a facilitator, mentor, and guide. Teachers create a supportive learning environment, offer guidance when needed, and ensure students have the resources and tools to succeed. The teacher's expertise is utilized to design meaningful learning experiences and provide targeted support to individual students. This approach values students' uniqueness, prior knowledge, and personal interests. It encourages collaboration, critical thinking, and self-directed learning. The goal is to create an environment where students are engaged, motivated, and empowered to take ownership of their learning outcomes.

The advantages of a student-centered classroom are numerous and far-reaching. One of the key benefits is increased student engagement. When students have a say in what they learn and how they know it, their interest and enthusiasm naturally rise. This engagement leads to better retention of information and a deeper understanding of concepts. Furthermore, a student-centered approach cultivates critical thinking skills. Students are encouraged to ask questions, explore ideas, and analyze information independently. This enhances their cognitive abilities and prepares them to be lifelong learners.

In a student-centered classroom, differentiation becomes a fundamental practice. Educators tailor instruction to meet the individual needs and abilities of each student. This personalization acknowledges learners' varying learning styles, paces, and strengths. By making decisions about their learning, students become more self-directed and motivated learners.

A student-centered classroom emphasizes collaboration rather than competition. Group projects, discussions, and peer evaluations encourage students to collaborate, share ideas, and learn from one another. These collaborative experiences mirror real-world scenarios where teamwork is essential. Cooperative learning also enhances communication skills and prepares students for the collaborative nature of the modern workforce.

A student-centered classroom has the potential to revolutionize education. It aligns with the demands of the 21st century, where critical thinking, problem-solving, and adaptability are paramount. Moreover, it equips students with the skills they need to navigate a rapidly changing world. As more educators embrace student-centered practices, we can expect to see a shift in educational outcomes, with students becoming more independent, motivated, and prepared for the challenges of higher education and the workforce.

By placing students at the center of the educational process, we empower them to become active participants, critical thinkers, and lifelong learners. As educators, administrators, and policymakers embrace the principles of a student-centered approach, they pave the way for a transformative shift in education that prepares students for success in a complex and interconnected world.

We have gone through 30K words and hundreds of ideas and the book can be summed up in two big thoughts:

1. Starting with the students at the center will empower learners.
2. Your visit to a lemonade stand might inspire other kids who witness it to pursue their creative ideas and entrepreneurial ventures. Stopping at a lemonade stand is a small gesture that can significantly impact young lives, fostering learning, creativity, confidence, and community engagement.

Both points encourage win-win interactions that spread positivity and support.

Building a Student-Centered Classroom

About the Author

Dr. Matthew X. Joseph is the Assistant Superintendent of Teaching and Learning in New Bedford MA. He is also the CEO of X-Factor EDU consulting and publishing. Experiences such as Executive Director of Teaching and Learning, Director of Curriculum and Instruction, Director of Digital Learning and Innovation, elementary school principal, classroom teacher, and district professional development specialist have provided Matt with incredible insights on how to best support teaching and learning and led to nationally published articles and opportunities to speak at multiple state and national events. His master's degree is in special education and his Ed.D. in Educational Leadership from Boston College. He is the author of Power Of Connections: Connecting Educators, Cultivating Professional Learning Networks, & Redefining Educator Collaboration, Stronger Together: The Power of Connections in a School Community, co-author of Disrupt The Status Quo, and co-author of Modern Mentoring, Reimagining Mentorship in Education. Follow him on Twitter @matthewxjoseph, visit his website at xfactor.link He is the author of three books focused on collaboration in education. Follow him on Twitter @matthewxjoseph

#StrongerTogether

About the Editor

Sarah Laliberte has worked as a writer and editor in the publishing industry for over 18 years. She brings a passion for words to her writing and editing in order to create clear and engaging content. Sarah enjoys helping other writers bring their writing into focus, and she aims to share information and ideas in a way that tickles readers' brains. Sarah is an alumni of the North Carolina School of Science and Mathematics and the University of North Carolina at Chapel Hill. She currently lives in the Blue Ridge Mountains of North Carolina.

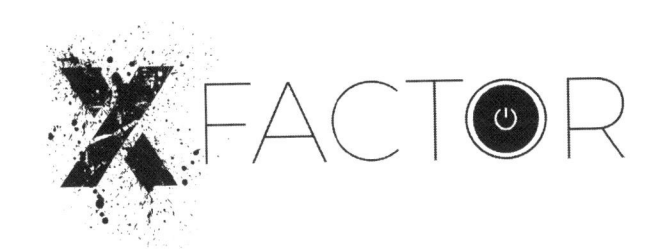

View our services, catalog of books, and meet our team of authors at https://xfactoredu.org.

Our team of educators are using their voice, journey, experiences, and practices to be the catalyst for change in education.

Visit: https://xfactoredu.org

Leadership Series

Kid Series

X FACTOR

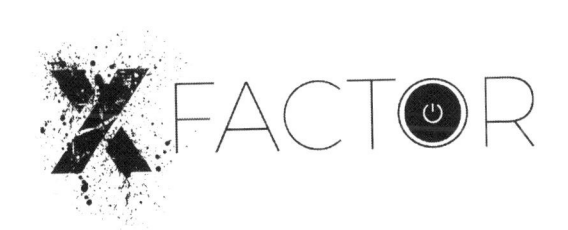

Made in the USA
Middletown, DE
02 October 2023